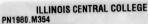
63084

PN   Mahlmann, Lewis.
1980
.M354 Puppet plays from
            favorite stories

PN
1980   Mahlmann,   63084
.M354   Puppet plays from
                 favorite stories

CA ED NOV 20 79 DEISSLER
MAR   I 12924
SEP 29 80
OCT 14 82   I 10363
CA ED DEC 5 83 Dressler H 2968940
CAR ED DEC 5 84 Deissler I F 2569
                                         I F 3042

DATE   BORROWER'S NAME

© THE BAKER & TAYLOR CO.

PUPPET PLAYS
from
FAVORITE STORIES

Puppet Plays
from
Favorite Stories

18 royalty-free plays
for hand puppets,
rod puppets or marionettes

by

LEWIS MAHLMANN

AND

DAVID CADWALADER JONES

With a Foreword by Burr Tillstrom

Publishers   PLAYS, INC.   *Boston*

Library of Congress Cataloging in Publication Data

Mahlmann, Lewis.
  Puppet plays from favorite stories.

  CONTENTS: Cinderella. — The pied piper of hamelin. — Puss-in-boots. — Rumpelstiltskin. [etc.]
  1. Puppets and puppet-plays. [1. Puppets and puppet-plays] I. Jones, David Cadwalader, joint author. II. Title.
PN1980.M354   791.5'38   77-23548
ISBN 0-8238-0219-1

Contents

Preface

Here is our second book of puppet plays, eighteen of them, that have been written for all those who are "young at heart." Our first book, *Puppet Plays for Young Players,* has been well received, so we felt that another book of puppet plays, successfully produced at the Storybook Theater in Children's Fairyland Park, Oakland, California, would be helpful to those interested in the puppet theater.

Some of these plays are easy to do. Others are more complicated and elaborate. All the plays, as in our first book, are adaptable for performance by live actors. A helpful chapter on producing puppet plays, making puppets, constructing a stage and settings, and manipulating hand puppets and marionettes may be found in *Puppet Plays for Young Players.*

The plays in this book have been a challenge to write, but they are, we feel, good theater for all ages. Read through them. Perhaps they will suggest other favorite tales you would like to do. By reading these different kinds of stories in play form, you will start to understand how a story is developed into exciting theater.

Fairy tales, folktales, and legends will always be popular, and the puppet theater brings them to life for easy understanding. Try your hand at making this important literature come alive for the young.

LEWIS MAHLMANN
DAVID CADWALADER JONES

Foreword

Here's another book of puppet plays by my friends, Lewis Mahlmann and David Jones. If you enjoyed *Puppet Plays for Young Players* as much as I did, I know you'll be as happy as I am with their new book.

Nothing has been more rewarding to me throughout my career as a puppeteer than the laughter and enthusiasm of a happy audience. These new plays will give you many wonderful opportunities to entertain audiences of all ages and to be rewarded as I have been by their enthusiastic response. Get your puppets, learn your lines, paint the scenery, rehearse well, turn on the stage lights, pull the curtain and have fun!

BURR TILLSTROM
Kukla, Fran, and Ollie

PUPPET PLAYS
from
FAVORITE STORIES

CINDERELLA

Characters

NARRATOR
CINDERELLA
LENA, *the skinny sister*
FATIMA, *the fat sister*
STEPMOTHER
OSCAR, *the page*
PRINCE CHARMING
FAIRY GODMOTHER

SCENE 1

SETTING: *The kitchen, with large fireplace.*
AT RISE: FATIMA *and* LENA *are rummaging through a trunk, tossing clothes about.*

NARRATOR: There were once three girls who lived with their stern mother in a little house not far from Prince Charming's castle. The oldest was Lena, who was too skinny and vain. The second was her sister, Fatima, who was too fat and clumsy. And the third was their stepsister, Cinderella. She was beautiful, good, and kind. Cinderella's father had remarried, bringing his new wife and her two daughters into the house, and no more than a year went by when he died. Cinderella's stepmother and stepsisters mistreated her and made her do all the nasty and heavy work in the house.

LENA: Where is Cinderella? I have work for her to do. There is a rumor that the Prince is having a ball tonight and all the beautiful girls of the town will be invited. I must get ready.

FATIMA: Why would he invite you? You are too skinny. He wouldn't look at you. He likes them well-rounded — like me!

LENA: Well-rounded? *Fat* is the word — *Fat*ima.

FATIMA: And you are nothing but skin and bones, Lena. You are ugly!

LENA: Ugly, am I? I'll make you eat your words!

FATIMA: You had better start eating something . . . skinny!

LENA: You fathead!

FATIMA: Skinny! (*They argue and fight.*)

STEPMOTHER (*Entering*): Girls, girls, shame on you! Arguing like that. You should act like ladies at all times. And set an example for your stepsister, Cinderella. Be gentle! (*Calls coarsely*) *Cinderella!*

CINDERELLA (*Entering*): Yes, ma'am.

STEPMOTHER: Come here at once. You haven't picked up after your sisters yet. Look at this mess!

FATIMA: What a lazy good-for-nothing!

CINDERELLA: But I've scrubbed all the floors, washed the breakfast dishes, made the beds and . . .

STEPMOTHER: Well, that's a start. But you had better hurry up and finish your morning chores. I've more for you to do.

LENA: And you must sew this tear in my sleeve.

FATIMA: And don't forget to bake those raspberry tarts! Yum, yum. (*There is a knock on door.*)

STEPMOTHER (*Annoyed*): Now who could that be?

LENA: The Prince has come to ask me to the ball.

FATIMA: No, to ask me!

LENA: No, me, you pig! (*They argue.* CINDERELLA *opens the door and* OSCAR *enters.*)

STEPMOTHER (*Warningly*): Girls! (*To* OSCAR) Ahhh! Welcome to our loving home, good page.

OSCAR: Good afternoon, ma'am. And good afternoon, ladies.

LENA *and* FATIMA: How do you do! (*Laughing*) Tee-hee! (LENA *and* FATIMA *stand in front of* CINDERELLA.)

OSCAR: His Highness, Prince Charming, has invited all the eligible young ladies of the countryside to a fancy dress ball tonight. All your daughters are invited, ma'am.

STEPMOTHER: They would love to come. Wouldn't you, girls?

FATIMA: Oh, yes.

LENA: Of course.

CINDERELLA: Oh, yes.

LENA (*To* CINDERELLA): *Not* you, stupid!

OSCAR: *All* eligible girls are invited.

STEPMOTHER: We understand, good page.

OSCAR: Well, goodbye, until tonight.

ALL: Goodbye! (*They curtsy and* OSCAR *exits.*)

LENA: I knew it. The Prince is anxious to meet me. I'm so glad I have a new dress for tonight. I'll start dressing now so that I'll be ready in time. I'll be so beautiful — in no time at all.

FATIMA: It will take longer than that to make *you* beautiful. Ha! More like a week! (*Laughs*)

LENA: A week? You will *never* get ready in time.

FATIMA: I'll start right away. Cinderella! Quick, get my dress — and my wig. Step on it!

LENA: Your wig won't look any better if she steps on it — not on *your* head. No, Cinderella, get my things first — my veils, my feathers.

CINDERELLA: I have nothing to wear. May I borrow . . . ?

STEPMOTHER: What? You don't think you are going, do you?

FATIMA (*Laughing*): Cinderella thinks she's going to the ball. The Prince certainly wouldn't look at her.

LENA: Not in those rags she wears.

STEPMOTHER: Someone must stay at home and watch the house. Besides, you won't have your chores done by tonight. Now, help your sisters get ready. (*She exits.*)

LENA: My veils, rouge and powder —

FATIMA: No, Cinderella. My comb —

CINDERELLA: Yes, sister.

LENA: No — me first!

FATIMA: Me first! (*They argue and rush about. Curtain*)

*   *   *   *   *

SCENE 2

SETTING: *The same as Scene 1.*

AT RISE: CINDERELLA *is sitting beside fireplace, sobbing.*

NARRATOR: And so the two vain sisters and their wicked mother got ready for the Prince's ball — with Cinderella's help. Cinderella was left sitting in the ashes and sobbing, because she was left behind.

CINDERELLA (*Crying*): But why couldn't I have gone? There are plenty of gowns in my stepsisters' closets that they never wear. Perhaps I *am* too plain — and the Prince would never look at me. But I would have liked to have gone anyway. (FAIRY GODMOTHER *appears.*)

GODMOTHER: Cinderella! Cinderella! Why do you cry? It sounds as if your heart would break.

CINDERELLA (*Startled*): Oh! Excuse me, but you startled me. How did you know my name?

GODMOTHER: I am your Fairy Godmother. I heard you crying. May I help you? What is wrong?

CINDERELLA: There is a ball tonight. The Prince has invited all the girls of the countryside, but I must stay at home and tend the house.

GODMOTHER: Nonsense! The house can tend itself. We'll see that you go.

CINDERELLA: But how? I've nothing to wear!

GODMOTHER: We'll fix that! (*She waves her magic wand and* CINDERELLA *is dressed in a beautiful gown. See Production Notes for change.*)

CINDERELLA: It's magic. This gown is so beautiful!

GODMOTHER (*Holding up clear slippers*): And here are your dancing slippers, made of glass.

CINDERELLA: Thank you, Fairy Godmother. But I've no way to get to the ball.

GODMOTHER (*Producing mice, lizards and pumpkin*): Here are some mice for horses, two lizards for coachmen and a pumpkin for the coach. Now watch! (*They are changed into coach, horses and coachmen. See Production Notes for change.*)

CINDERELLA: Oh, how can I thank you?

GODMOTHER: By promising to leave the ball before the clock strikes the hour of midnight. (CINDERELLA *gets into coach.*)

CINDERELLA: I promise. (*Waving*) Thank you! Thank you!

GODMOTHER: Have a good time. (*Curtain*)

*   *   *   *   *

SCENE 3

SETTING: *The courtyard in front of the castle, with steps leading to the castle door. A large clock face is on the wall.*

AT RISE: OSCAR *comes out of castle, then the* PRINCE.

NARRATOR: It was already late when Cinderella set out for the ball. At the castle, Oscar opened the doors for the dancing couples to cool themselves in the night air.

PRINCE: It's much cooler out here.

OSCAR: Are you having a good time at your ball, Prince?

PRINCE (*Half-heartedly*): I guess so. But it's just too stuffy in there.

OSCAR: Have you found a pretty maid among all your guests? One that might be your bride?

PRINCE: They are either too plain or too fussy. Too tall or too short. And there are two sisters with their mother, one *much* too skinny and the other *much* too fat. And all three are so vain! I'm sure that each thinks that she will be the next queen.

OSCAR: I remember them. I wonder where the third sister is? As I remember, she was most beautiful.

PRINCE: I haven't seen anyone like that.

OSCAR: I had better look after the guests. Please excuse me, Prince. (OSCAR *exits.*)

PRINCE: Surely there must be one for me among them. All the maidens of the neighboring towns were invited.

CINDERELLA (*Appearing*): Oh, excuse me, sir. I'm afraid I'm late.

PRINCE: I'm sure the Prince would welcome a beautiful lady such as you at any time. Let me take you inside. Won't you dance with me?

CINDERELLA: Oh, thank you, sir. I would be most delighted. (*They exit together. Stage is empty and music is heard.* LENA *and* FATIMA *enter, in ball gowns.*)

LENA: Did you see her? Who was that Princess dancing with the Prince?

FATIMA: Pretty dress, but *such* a plain girl. The Prince will never give her another look.

LENA: I didn't see him look at you a second time after you
were introduced.

FATIMA: He barely said hello to you. Probably he could
barely see you, you are so skinny, Lena!

LENA: Well, he would have no trouble seeing you, *Fatima*.
(*They argue.*)

STEPMOTHER (*Appearing*): Girls! Girls! (*They stop arguing*) Don't fight until you get home. The Prince might get
the wrong impression.

FATIMA: It seems the impressions are being made by that
... that ...

STEPMOTHER: She seems familiar. But no! Come back inside. We will put you girls in the front row again. Perhaps the Prince will ask one of you to dance.

LENA: *Me!*

FATIMA: No, *me!* (*They argue again as they exit. Music
continues.* CINDERELLA *and* PRINCE *appear.*)

PRINCE: Please dance one more dance with me. I find you
beautiful and charming.

CINDERELLA: I would love to. (*They start to dance. Clock
hands move to midnight and clock begins to strike
twelve.*) But no! I must go!

PRINCE: But you just got here. You mustn't ...

CINDERELLA: The time! It's almost midnight.

PRINCE: But tonight is a special night.

CINDERELLA: I must go! Please!

PRINCE: You didn't tell me your name.

CINDERELLA: The time is almost up ... oh! (*She starts off*)

PRINCE: Wait!

CINDERELLA: Goodbye, my prince. (*She runs off.*)

PRINCE (*Calling after her*): Princess! Oh, she's gone. But
look! She left one of her glass slippers. (*Holds up glass
slipper. Curtain*)

*   *   *   *   *

SCENE 4

SETTING: *Same as Scene 1.*
AT RISE: *Stage is empty.*

NARRATOR: Cinderella rushed back to the little house, as the coach disappeared and a pumpkin rolled into the gutter. The horses changed back to mice and scampered away. The coachmen turned back into lizards. When Cinderella got home, she was in her old tattered dress again. Lena and Fatima came home long after, still talking about the ball. (LENA *and* FATIMA *come in.*)

FATIMA: Wasn't the Prince handsome? He winked at me.

LENA: He probably had something in his eye. He brushed against my skirt as he danced by me.

FATIMA: I saw you stand in his way. (*They argue again.*)

STEPMOTHER (*Entering*): Girls! Girls! Not again. You'll never get a husband, let alone a prince, by arguing. Be sweet like me. (*Loud and demanding*) Cinderella! *Cinderella!* Get in here *at once!*

CINDERELLA (*Entering, in tattered dress*): I was just washing the attic windows.

STEPMOTHER: When I call you, I want you to come at once. Do you understand?

LENA: She's always late when we call her, too.

STEPMOTHER: Just what are you mooning about, girl? You'd think it was you who went to the ball last night, instead of my pretty girls.

FATIMA: Cinderella . . . at the ball? (*Laughs*)

LENA: She'd be a fine one at the Prince's ball. (*Laughs*) She's so clumsy.

STEPMOTHER: Cinderella, I have many things for you to do today. First, clean out the pigsty.

CINDERELLA: Yes, Stepmother. (*She exits.*)

FATIMA: You just have to start making her behave, Mother dear. (*There is a knock on the door*)

LENA: It's the Prince coming for me. I'll get it.

FATIMA: I'll get it. (*They push each other.*)

STEPMOTHER: I'll get it! (*She lets* OSCAR *in. He has glass slipper on a pillow.*)

OSCAR: His Highness, the Prince!

LENA *and* FATIMA: Oh-h-h!

STEPMOTHER: Girls, please. (PRINCE *enters*) Good day, Your Highness.

LENA: My Highness.

LENA *and* FATIMA: Our Highness. (*They curtsy.*)

STEPMOTHER: We must tell you how we enjoyed your ball.

PRINCE: I've come in search of a girl ... *the* girl for me. She dropped her glass slipper last night as she ran down the steps.

LENA (*Quickly*): I lost my slipper last night.

FATIMA (*Quickly*): So did I!

PRINCE: Whoever fits this shoe will be my bride.

LENA: I'm sure it's mine. Let me try it on.

STEPMOTHER: Yes. It looks like yours, dear. Page, over here. (OSCAR *kneels in front of* LENA) Now just slip your foot into that sweet little glass slipper, Lena. It does look like the one you lost.

FATIMA: Humph!

LENA: Yes, it does. (*She groans and grunts, trying to put shoe on. See Production Notes regarding trying on of shoe.*) My foot seems to have swelled a bit from last night.

FATIMA: Those clod hoppers couldn't get into that little shoe for anything — at any time!

OSCAR: The lady's foot does seem a bit too long.

FATIMA: Yes, about a foot too long. (*Laughs*)

PRINCE: Perhaps we had better ...

STEPMOTHER: Fatima! Didn't you say you had lost your slipper, too? Page, let the other girl try.

OSCAR: Yes, ma'am. (*He kneels in front of* FATIMA)

FATIMA: I'd recognize my shoe anywhere. Now to put it on. . . . (*She, too, grunts and groans trying to put shoe on.*)

LENA: If she gets one toe in, she's lucky.

STEPMOTHER: Lena, hush!

FATIMA: Ouch! Help me, Lena.

LENA: Why don't you try putting it on sideways?

OSCAR: I'm afraid the shoe might break, Your Highness.

PRINCE: We had better go on to the next house. (CINDER-ELLA *enters.*)

CINDERELLA: Stepmother, I've finished cleaning.

STEPMOTHER: Get out! *Get out!*

PRINCE: And who is this?

FATIMA: The scrub woman!

LENA: The maid!

STEPMOTHER: My stepdaughter. You are excused, Cinderella.

CINDERELLA: But that shoe is . . .

STEPMOTHER: Get out!

PRINCE (*To* CINDERELLA): But you haven't tried on the glass slipper yet.

LENA: Cinderella? (*Laughs*)

STEPMOTHER: This one was home safe by the fireplace last night.

CINDERELLA: Let me try, Stepmother.

STEPMOTHER: Get out, girl!

GODMOTHER (*Appearing*): Let her try, my good woman!

STEPMOTHER: How dare you!

PRINCE (*To* CINDERELLA): Please try on the shoe, my dear. (OSCAR *kneels in front of* CINDERELLA. *She slips the shoe onto her foot.*)

SISTERS *and* STEPMOTHER: The slipper fits!

GODMOTHER: Yes. This *is* Cinderella's shoe. And Cinderella *did* attend the ball last night.

STEPMOTHER: Impossible!

GODMOTHER: You shall see! (*She waves her wand and* CIN-DERELLA *magically changes into her beautiful ball gown as in Scene 2.*)

LENA *and* FATIMA: Oh, no!

STEPMOTHER: It can't be!

PRINCE: It's the same girl. The girl for me! (*He goes to her*) Will you marry me?

CINDERELLA: Yes. And love you with all my heart.

LENA *and* FATIMA: Oh-h-h! (*They faint.*)

NARRATOR: And so the Prince married Cinderella and they all lived happily — except for Lena and Fatima — ever after. (*Curtain*)

THE END

Production Notes

CINDERELLA

Number of Puppets: 10 hand or rod puppets or marionettes. (3 are costume-change puppets for Cinderella and
sisters.)

Characters: 1 male or female for Narrator.

Playing Time: 15 minutes.

Description of Puppets: Cinderella wears ragged clothes
and changes into ball gown (see Special Effects). Sisters
also change into ball gowns. Fatima should be fat and
Lena tall and thin. Godmother could be a half-size puppet with wings or an old lady with a pointed hat. Look at
illustrations in books of fairy tales for costume ideas, and
use your imagination.

Properties: Trunk with clothes, wand, glass slippers and
glass slipper attached to fancy pillow; mice, lizards and
pumpkin and coach, horses and coachmen, which can
be flat cut-outs.

Setting: Scenes 1, 2 and 4: The kitchen. There is a large
fireplace. Scene 3: The castle courtyard, with steps leading to the castle door. A large clock face, with hands
pointing nearly to midnight, is on the wall. The clock
might have hands that move toward midnight during
scene. Dancers might be visible through castle windows.

Lighting: Kitchen is bright for Scenes 1 and 4, and dim for
Scene 2. Courtyard is dim but with an offstage light il-
luminating the area.

Sound: Clock striking twelve, music (Prokofiev's *Cinderella*).

Special Effects: For magic change of Cinderella's clothes in a hand or rod puppet show, either have tattered dress over ball gown and quickly pull it off, or exchange puppets. In a marionette show, either exchange marionettes or use a "flip over" marionette with a head at each end, one long skirt ragged and the other fancy. For the magic change of pumpkin to coach, in hand or rod puppet show, use small pumpkin cut-out on a stick and exchange for large cut-out of coach and horses. For a marionette show, place the cut-out flat on the stage and bring up with strings (or it may be accordion-pleated so that it folds flat and can be attached to the front of the stage floor, where it is not seen until it is brought up with strings). When Cinderella loses her shoe in the courtyard, in a marionette show, either throw the shoe onstage, or release a shoe hidden under her skirt. In a hand or rod puppet show, simply have the Prince pick up the slipper from below for audience to see. To try on the shoe with hand or rod puppets, have Oscar hold the shoe and use a prop foot extended from under the skirt to try on shoe. In a marionette show, you can actually use the foot of the marionette. Cinderella can try on shoe without keeping it on her foot, since it is attached to the pillow.

THE PIED PIPER OF HAMELIN

From the poem by Robert Browning

Characters

MICHAEL RAT
UNCLE THEODORE RAT
FRITZ, *boy*
GERTY, *girl*
FRAU UBERNASE
DOCTOR SCHNITZEL
MAYOR GROSSMAN
PIED PIPER
HERMAN, *crippled boy*
RATS
CHILDREN

SCENE 1

BEFORE RISE: MICHAEL RAT *enters with a sack over his shoulder.*

MICHAEL (*Calling*): Uncle Theodore! (UNCLE THEODORE *enters. He carries old-fashioned ear trumpet.*)

UNCLE THEODORE: Yes, Michael? Are you ready to see the world?

MICHAEL: All ready. My sack is packed.

THEODORE: What? (*Holds up ear trumpet*)

MICHAEL (*Loudly*): I'm all ready to go.

THEODORE: Oh, yes. Well, you're old enough to sow your oats, young rat. Where are you going?

MICHAEL: I thought I'd go to Paris —

THEODORE (*Interrupting*): What?

MICHAEL (*Loudly*): I thought *Paris* — then London, to visit the King. But on my way, I'll stop in Hamelin Town.

THEODORE: What did you say? Oh, Paris — fine. London, O.K. But, by no means stop in Hamelin.

MICHAEL: Why not? Aren't you from Hamelin, Uncle?

THEODORE: Yes, but you must never go there. I lost my family in that place, and I would be dead, too, if I weren't hard of hearing.

MICHAEL: What happened?

THEODORE: Come, I'll tell you. (*They start to walk off.*) You see, long ago there was a plague of rats in Hamelin ... (*They exit.*)

*   *   *

TIME: *Long ago.*

SETTING: *Interior of Town Hall in Hamelin.*

AT RISE: RATS *are scampering all about. They hide as* FRITZ *enters.*

FRITZ: I'm going to hide and surprise Gerty. But where can I hide? (*Looks about, points to left corner.*) Over here will do. (*He runs to left corner and hides.*)

GERTY (*Entering, carrying a doll*): Where are you, Fritz? I know he's here somewhere. (*She looks around.*) Is he hiding in the corner? (*Looks into right corner*) No. Maybe over here. (*Runs center*)

FRITZ (*Jumping out*): Boo! (GERTY *jumps in fright.* FRITZ *laughs.*)

GERTY: Oh, I knew where you were all the time.

FRITZ: What will we play now?

GERTY: Let's count the panes in the Town Hall windows.

FRITZ: No. I can't count very high yet.

GERTY: We could play with my dolly. (*She holds up doll.*)

FRITZ: No, that's no fun. Let's look for more rats. There are rats here in the Town Hall, too. Aren't they funny? I think I'll catch one.

GERTY: Oh, ugh! Leave them alone. Mama says they are dirty things, hiding everywhere — even in our kitchen.

FRITZ: Oh, well, never mind. Let's find Herman and play outside. We're not supposed to be in the Town Hall, anyway.

GERTY: But there are more rats outside! (*Reluctantly*) Oh, all right. (*They exit. In a moment,* DOCTOR SCHNITZEL *and* FRAU UBERNASE *enter.*)

FRAU UBERNASE: Where is the Mayor? This rat situation is growing worse all the time. He simply must do something about it.

DOCTOR SCHNITZEL: Yes. There are rats in my desk, and my medicine cabinet, and everywhere! (MAYOR GROSS-MAN *enters.*)

MAYOR GROSSMAN: Good afternoon, Frau Ubernase, Doctor Schnitzel.

FRAU: Good afternoon, indeed! You promised to rid us of the horrible rats in this town.

DOCTOR: Yes. You are the Mayor. You promised!

MAYOR: I've had traps set, and poison put out . . .

FRAU: Yes — and the rats spring the traps without getting caught, and grow fat on the poisoned barley.

DOCTOR: They are running away with our town. We are being eaten out of house and home!

MAYOR: What can we do? What can I do? (PIED PIPER *enters, carrying flute.*)

PIED PIPER: Good day, Herr Mayor.

MAYOR: Who are you, and what do you want here?

PIPER: I am the Pied Piper.

FRAU: With all our troubles, the last thing we need is music.

DOCTOR: Off with you. We have enough pests as it is.

PIPER: Perhaps I can help you. I see you have rat problems.

MAYOR: Too many rat problems.

PIPER: Perhaps I can solve your dilemma.

MAYOR, FRAU *and* DOCTOR (*Ad lib; excitedly*): How? What do you mean? Tell us! (*Etc.*)

PIPER: Pay me one thousand guilders and I'll rid Hamelin Town of all its rats.

MAYOR: We'll pay you five thousand guilders if you can do that.

DOCTOR: Oh, yes. Anything!

FRAU: Please help!

PIED PIPER: One thousand guilders will be fine. Tomorrow all the rats will be gone. So, until tomorrow — goodbye. (*He quickly exits.*)

FRAU: Our hero. (*She exits.*)

DOCTOR SCHNITZEL: What a genius. (*He exits.*)

MAYOR: Hmm. Let's wait and see. (*Follows them off. Curtain.*)

*   *   *   *   *

SCENE 2

TIME: *Next day.*

SETTING: *Street in Hamelin. Backdrop shows Bavarian-style buildings.*

AT RISE: RATS *are scampering about, as* FRITZ *and* GERTY *enter.*

FRITZ: What shall we play? Pin the tail on the rat?

GERTY: That's not funny. Oh, Fritz, let's go home. There are just too many rats out here. (*She runs off.*)

FRITZ (*Calling after her*): Don't let them bother you. (HER-

MAN, *the crippled boy, limps onstage with his crutch under one arm*) Hi, Herman. Want to play ball?

HERMAN: I can't catch with this crutch. Come over to my house, and we'll have something to eat, instead.

FRITZ: Good idea. I'm sorry you have to use that crutch, Herman. (*They exit, arm in arm.* FRAU *and* DOCTOR *enter.*)

FRAU: He should start soon. The Piper promised he would get rid of the rats by noon.

DOCTOR (*Pointing offstage*): Here comes the Mayor.

MAYOR (*Entering*): Good morning, everybody.

DOCTOR: Where is he? Where is the Piper?

MAYOR: He's on his way. Let's go to the edge of the river and watch the rats disappear. (*All exit.* PIPER *enters, with flute.*)

PIPER: Now's the time. Here's my pipe to play.... (*Plays pipe and dances about. Flute music is heard from off-stage.* RATS *start to enter.* PIPER *dances in a circle, with* RATS *following, then exits.* RATS *follow him off, and other* RATS *enter and cross the stage, following* PIPER *off.*)

MAYOR (*From offstage*): Look! Here they come!

DOCTOR (*From offstage*): Stand aside, everyone.

FRAU (*From offstage*): Look! They are entering the water by the dozens. (*More* RATS *cross stage.*)

MAYOR, FRAU *and* DOCTOR (*From offstage, cheering*): Hooray! (*Last* RATS *cross stage and exit. Music stops.* MAYOR, FRAU *and* DOCTOR *enter.* MAYOR *is carrying small bag.*)

MAYOR: Three cheers for the Pied Piper! (PIPER *enters.*)

DOCTOR, MAYOR *and* FRAU: Hooray! Hooray! Hooray!

PIPER: Thanks for your bravos, but I must be on my way. Just give me my one thousand guilders and I'll be gone.

MAYOR: Pay that sum to a wandering gypsy? Never. Our business together is done, Piper.

DOCTOR: We're not ones to shirk from duty, but one thousand guilders . . .

FRAU: Our losses have made us thrifty.

MAYOR (*Handing* PIPER *bag*): Here — take fifty guilders.

PIPER: Folks who cheat me may find me piping to another tune.

MAYOR (*Getting angry*): That's all you'll get!

FRAU: Take that or nothing at all.

PIPER: One thousand — a bargain is a bargain. . . .

DOCTOR: Off with you, and never return.

MAYOR: Or we will chase you away. You — threaten us? Do your worst! Blow your pipe, there, till you burst! Now, get out of here. (*They exit, leaving* PIPER *alone.*)

PIPER (*Calling after them*): Don't say I didn't warn you! (*He plays flute. Music is heard from offstage.* FRITZ *and* GERTY *enter.*)

GERTY: Listen to that beautiful music. It seems to be calling me.

FRITZ: Look at that funny-looking piper. Let's follow him. (*Calls offstage*) Come on, everybody. Come follow the Pied Piper and let's see where he will go. (CHILDREN *enter.* GERTY *and* FRITZ *follow* PIPER *offstage, and* CHILDREN *follow them off. Finally* HERMAN *enters, leaning on his crutch.*)

HERMAN: Wait for me! (*Crosses slowly and exits. Curtain.*)

*   *   *   *   *

SCENE 3

SETTING: *In front of Koppelberg Hill. This scene is played before curtain.*

AT RISE: PIPER, *still playing, leads* FRITZ, GERTY *and* CHILDREN *in from one side of stage and exits with them through curtain, into Koppelberg Hill.* MICHAEL *and* THEODORE *enter.*

THEODORE: And so, the Piper led all the children of Hamelin into the base of Koppelberg Hill with the magic of his piping. It was as if they were under a spell. (HERMAN *enters slowly, on his crutch.*)

MICHAEL: Here comes Herman, the crippled boy. Does he go into the mountain, too?

HERMAN (*Calling*): Wait for me! (*Offstage music stops.*) Where am I? Why am I here — in front of Koppelberg Hill? Where are my friends? I must have been in a trance. I'd better go home now. (*Turns and slowly exits.*)

MICHAEL: What happened to the children?

THEODORE: They were never seen again.

MICHAEL: How do you know all this, Uncle Theodore?

THEODORE: I was there. You see, I was hard of hearing then, also, and could not hear the music of the Pied Piper. Now, off you go. Have a good time, Michael.

MICHAEL: Goodbye, Uncle. (*Starts off, waving*) Goodbye! (*Exits*)

THEODORE (*Waving*): Goodbye! (*Exits in opposite direction.*)

THE END

Production Notes

THE PIED PIPER OF HAMELIN

Number of Puppets: 9 hand or rod puppets, and cut-outs of Rats and Children on rods.

Playing Time: 10 minutes.

Description of Puppets: Frau, Doctor, Mayor, Fritz and Gerty are dressed in old German costumes. A rod puppet would be especially good for the Pied Piper, who should be tall and skinny. He wears long coat, half yellow and half red, has blue eyes and a merry smile. His hands should be attached to the flute with a string that pulls the flute up to his mouth when he plays. Michael and Uncle Theodore should look like mice, with old German hats and jackets (optional). Herman has a crutch attached under his arm.

Properties: Small bag, doll, old-fashioned ear trumpet.

Setting: Scene 1, Interior of Town Hall in Hamelin, painted on backdrop. Scene 2, Street, with Bavarian buildings painted on backdrop. Scene 3, Koppelberg Hill, painted on the front curtain, divided in the middle to let Piper and Children enter.

Lighting: No special effects.

Sound: Offstage flute or recorder music, as indicated in text.

PUSS-IN-BOO

From the story by Charles Perrau

Characters

PETER, *a miller's son*
PUSS-IN-BOOTS
KING
COOK
PRINCESS
OGRE
LION
MOUSE

SCENE 1

TIME: *Long ago.*
SETTING: *In front of the mill that is Peter's home.*
AT RISE: PETER *is onstage, looking for his cat.*

PETER: Here, Puss! Here, kitty! Where can he have gone? And why did Papa leave me only a cat? I've probably lost that now. John got the mill and my brother George the donkey, but me.... just Puss. Oh, well. I should be grateful for that. He's such a nice cat. I wonder where he is? And what do you think he wanted with those coins? They were all I had.
PUSS: Hello, there, Master. (PUSS-IN-BOOTS, *a handsome cat, in fancy dress, enters.*)

TER: Puss . . . Look at you! Where did you get all those fine clothes? A big red hat — a fancy blue cape — and those boots. What beautiful red boots! You didn't spend the last of my money on them, did you?

PUSS: Don't worry, Peter. You'll soon have plenty to eat, and you'll be dressed and treated like a king! (*He bows and curtsies.*) How do you do?

PETER: What are you doing?

PUSS: I'm practicing my manners.

PETER: Whatever for?

PUSS: To visit the King!

PETER: To visit the King? Did you say visit the King? But, why?

PUSS: Our King is very fond of partridge and rabbit, I understand.

PETER: Yes. That's true. But he complains that his hunters can't catch them. I hear that he seldom gets any to eat.

PUSS: And that is where I come in.

PETER: What do you mean?

PUSS: The King would pay a handsome price for a bagful, I dare say.

PETER: Most likely.

PUSS: I know a forest full of game. Have you ever seen a cat who wasn't a good hunter? Go home and I will meet you there later.

PETER: All right, Puss. Best of luck!

PUSS: Good luck to us both! (*They exit. Curtain.*)

*   *   *   *   *

SCENE 2

TIME: *A few hours later.*
SETTING: *The kitchen in the King's palace.*
AT RISE: KING *enters.*

KING: Oh, I'm so-o-o hungry! Where is that cook? I haven't had a rabbit or a partridge for so long! At night I dream of delicious cooked rabbit, fit for a king . . . that's me . . . all fixed with stuffing, and (*Rabbit on platter floats by.*) — what's that? I'm seeing things. Yum, yum! (*Tries to catch it*) Oh! (*It disappears.*) Where did it go? Fiddlesticks! Oh . . . just one little bite of a fancy roast partridge with figs and cherries. . . . I'd give anything if. . . . (*Partridge floats by.*) There's one! (*Tries to catch it, but it disappears, too*) I'm famished. I'm seeing things. They were both mirages. Where is that cook? I think I'm losing my mind. (*Calls*) Cook! Come here at once!

COOK (*Running in*): Yes, Your Majesty?

KING: Have my hunters returned from the fields?

COOK: Yes, Your Majesty.

KING: And what's for dinner?

COOK: Porridge, Your Majesty.

KING: Porridge! Now what kind of dish is that to set before a king? (*Aside*) Seems as if I've heard that line before. Porridge! I'm sick of porridge! What else do you have?

COOK: The hunters came back empty-handed. How about a nice roast cat?

KING: Cat?

COOK: Yes, one with red boots on just came to the back door. He says he wants to see you.

KING: A cat to see me? Send him in at once.

COOK: Yes, Your Majesty. (COOK *exits.*)

KING (*Shouting after him*): And no more porridge! If I have one more bowl of porridge or one more pie of blackbirds that keep squawking at me, I'll scream. Of course I don't mind those fiddlers playing while I eat, but that isn't very nourishing.

PUSS (*Entering with a bag of rabbits and partridges*): Your Majesty! My master, the Marquis of Carabas, sends you his humblest greetings and wishes to present to you this bag of rabbits and partridges. (*Lays bag before* KING)

KING: I accept his greetings and I am overjoyed with his gift. A whole bag of partridges and rabbits. Oh, joy! Goody, goody! (*To* PUSS) Thank the Marquis of. . . . What did you say his name was?

PUSS: The Marquis of Carabas.

KING: Yes, the Marquis of Carabas. Know him well! Thank him for me. What a wonderful gift! And give him this little token of my appreciation. Here is a bag of gold coins. (*Gets bag of coins and presents it to* PUSS)

PUSS (*Bowing*): Yes, Your Majesty. Thank you. Your Majesty is most generous. Good day, sir.

KING (*Calling*): Cook! Cook! (*To* PUSS) Oh, yes . . . Good day, Pussycat.

PUSS (*Aside, to audience*): Pussycat? Really! (*Exits with bag of coins.*)

KING: Cook! And now for a wonderful feast. (COOK *runs in.*) Look! (*Shows bag. Curtain.*)

*   *   *   *   *

SCENE 3

TIME: *A few minutes later.*
SETTING: *A spot by the side of a road, in front of a stream.*
AT RISE: PETER *is onstage.*

PETER: I wonder when Puss-in-Boots will return from the palace. Do you think he saw the King? I hope so.

PUSS (*Entering with bag*): Peter! Look what I have. A bag of gold! Here is the beginning of the fortune I promised you. (*Gives bag to* PETER.)

PETER: You did see the King. (*Looking into bag*) Hundreds of gold pieces. I can't believe it! You didn't steal these, did you?

PUSS: Oh, no. I just pleased the King with something for his stomach. You know, the way to a King's treasury is through his stomach.

PETER: Now I can get us a decent meal. And I can get a new suit . . . some fine clothes like yours, Puss. Then we can travel in style.

PUSS: No — wait. I have a plan to take care of that. This is only the beginning. Soon the King will be taking his daily ride by here. When you go for a swim, I'll hide your clothes, and when the King comes along. . . . Oh — I hear the coach. Go and get into the water.

PETER: What's going to happen?

PUSS: Do as I say.

PETER: All right. (PETER *exits.*)

PUSS: Oh, I'm so clever. Have you ever seen a cat as clever as I am? (*Suddenly alert*) Oh-oh. . . . Here come the King and his daughter now. (PUSS *exits.* KING*'s open coach comes in with* KING *and* PRINCESS *in it.*)

KING: Beautiful day for a ride, isn't it, my dear?

PRINCESS: Yes, Papa. Thank you for taking me out today. It is so lonely in that palace all by myself.

KING: One day you will find a handsome husband. We'll just keep looking.

PRINCESS: Oh, thank you, Papa.

PUSS (*Appearing, crying*): Boo-hoo. Boo-hoo.

KING: What's the matter, Pussycat?

PUSS: Oh, Your Majesty, my master, the Marquis of Carabas, has gone for a swim and some thieves have stolen his clothes. The Marquis can't come out of the water. Boo-hoo! He'll get sick if he stays in there any longer.

KING: I just happen to be coming back from the tailor, and I have a new suit that should fit the Marquis. Here. (*Hands box to* PUSS) Take it to him ... so he can dress.

PUSS: Oh, thank you, Your Majesty.

KING: Better hide your eyes, daughter.

PRINCESS: Oh, yes, Father. (*She covers her eyes.*)

KING: Oh, that poor boy. In that cold water. I hope he doesn't catch a chill.

PRINCESS: So do I, Papa. A marquis ... well! (PUSS *holds cape as if to conceal* PETER *as he dresses.* NOTE: *Offstage, the original* PETER *in shabby clothes is exchanged for another* PETER, *dressed in a regal suit of clothes, made of rich fabrics, with gold trim.*)

PUSS: The clothes are a perfect fit, Your Majesty. (*Takes down cape to reveal* PETER, *dressed as the Marquis, in his new finery.*)

KING: Perfect!

PRINCESS: I say!

PETER (*Bowing*): Your Majesty. These clothes are too good for me.

KING: Tut! Tut! Think nothing of it. I've many more where those came from. But do you think you might be able to get me another rabbit or partridge?

PETER: My friend, Puss-in-Boots, can get you more.

KING: What a clever cat!

PETER: So I find out.

KING: Oh, by the way ... This is my daughter, the Princess. Daughter — the Marquis of Carabas.

PRINCESS: How do you do!

PETER: My name is ...

PUSS (*Interrupting*): Your Majesty, the Marquis wishes you to visit his castle down the road to the South.

PETER: What?

KING: A castle too! I knew it! Oh, by all means.

PUSS: Just follow this road and it will take you there. I'll run ahead.

KING: Off we go. . . . Come sit next to the Princess, young man. I'm sure she will like that.

PRINCESS (*Embarrassed*): Oh, Papa! (*The coach leaves, with* KING, PETER, *and* PRINCESS.)

PUSS: Now to visit the wicked Ogre who lives in that castle down the road. I had better get there before Peter and the King do. The Ogre thinks he is a great magician, but we will see who is smarter. It is about time someone did something about him. He is so wicked, he steals princesses away from their homes and devours them. Just see what I will do to him! Now to get a fine home for my Marquis of Carabas, and a princess, too. (*He exits. Curtain.*)

*　　*　　*　　*　　*

SCENE 4

SETTING: *Inside the Ogre's castle.*

AT RISE: OGRE *is onstage, trying to do magic tricks.*

OGRE (*Waving hands and humming a sinister tune*): Dum-da-dum-dum. . . . (*To audience*) Welcome to my beautiful castle, everyone. I suppose you have come to see me do magic tricks. I am very clever, and I can do any kind of magic I want. Just to show you. . . . (*Gets box and puts it center*) Here is my magic box. Let's see what I can bring out. (*Chants*)

> Here I conjure and here I weave . . . .
> Now spooky spider do I perceive.
> Appear and show yourself right now —
> I'll wave my hand in this way — *pow!*

(*Gestures; nothing happens*) What did I do wrong? I had no trouble getting that beautiful maiden to appear yesterday. Of course, that wasn't really magic. I stole her from a farm nearby. She was delicious. (*Suddenly a spider appears from the box when the* OGRE *isn't looking, scaring him.*) Yikes! Where did that come from? Let's try something bigger. How about a cat? (*Chants*)

> Here I conjure and here I weave . . . .
> Now pussycat do I perceive.
> One so tender and tasty, too —
> One I make into a stew.

(*Gestures; again nothing happens*) Now what did I do wrong this time? Maybe I have to wait awhile. I won't look. (*He hides his eyes, as* PUSS-IN-BOOTS *enters.*)

PUSS: Good day, Ogre.

OGRE (*Seeing* PUSS): It worked! It worked! I don't have to go hunting for someone to eat today! Come to me, kitty. Don't run away.

PUSS: Who's running?

OGRE: Aren't you afraid of me? I'm a terrible magician.

PUSS: You can say that again. Ha!

OGRE: I am! I am! I am!

PUSS: I might be afraid of you if you were a ferocious lion, but I'm not afraid of a stupid ogre who thinks he's a magician.

OGRE: Well, I am a magician. And just to prove it, I'll turn myself into a lion. It would probably be more fun to eat you then, anyway. (*He becomes a* LION. *See Production Notes*) Grr-r-r! Are you scared now?

PUSS: Humph! Any magician can turn himself into a lion. But it takes a really clever one to turn himself into something as small as a mouse. I know you can't do that.

OGRE (*As* LION): I can! I can! I can! Just watch! (LION *turns into a small* MOUSE.) Now, see? I'm a little gray mouse, and I'm just as good a magician as anyone else.

PUSS: But not as smart or as fast as I am! (*He chases* MOUSE.)

OGRE (*As* MOUSE): Help! Squeak! Squeak!

PUSS (*Pouncing on* MOUSE *and downing it with one gulp*): I've got you! Mm-m-m. . . . Delicious. I had better clean up this castle. I hear the King coming, with the Princess and Peter. (*Races about, tidying castle, removing box, and finishes just as* KING, PETER *and* PRINCESS *enter.*) Welcome to the castle of the Marquis of Carabas. (*Bows*)

PETER: Really?

PUSS: Shh-h!

KING: So this is your castle.

PETER: I guess so.

KING: He's very modest. Daughter, I think I've found the man for you.

PRINCESS: I think so, too.

KING: Will you take the hand of my daughter, good Marquis?

PETER: Sure! Sounds great to me.

PRINCESS: Me, too! (*Giggles*)

KING: With a castle like this, and with your title, the Marquis of Carabas, I'm sure you both will be very happy.

PETER: I hope so, Your Majesty.

KING: Now let us start the arrangements for the marriage. (KING *and* PRINCESS *exit.*)

PETER: Puss-in-Boots, you were the best gift of all the presents from Papa. Thank you very much. (PETER *exits.*)

PUSS (*To audience*): And so the Marquis of Carabas and the King's daughter were married, and they all, except the Ogre, lived happily ever after. As for me, I was made the royal prime minister. (*Bows regally as curtain closes.*)

THE END

Production Notes

Puss-in-Boots

Number of Puppets: 9 hand puppets or marionettes; 1 is costume-change puppet for Peter in a period suit made of rich-looking cloth, with gold trim. The first Peter is dressed in shabby clothes.

Playing Time: 15 minutes.

Description of Puppets: Rich-looking clothes for King, Princess, and Peter, as described above. Puss-in-Boots has high red boots, large red hat with a plume, blue cape, etc. Cook has white apron and high white hat. Appropriate animal puppets for Lion and Mouse. Ogre should be made to look as grotesque and frightening as possible.

Properties: Rabbit, partridge, on platters (use cut-outs); sack, for Puss; bag of coins, for King; suit box; open coach (use a cut-out); spider; black magician's box.

Setting: There are four sets, and each should be shown by a representative drawing or cut-out on the backdrop. Scene 1, in front of the mill; Scene 2, kitchen in the palace; Scene 3, a spot by the side of a road, near a stream; Scene 4, the Ogre's castle.

Lighting: No special effects.

RUMPELSTILTSKIN

Characters

HUNTER
MILLER
KING
SARAH, *the Miller's daughter*
RUMPELSTILTSKIN
BABY

SCENE 1

SETTING: *The throne room in the palace. There is a throne at center, and there are banners and a tapestry decorating the stone walls.*

AT RISE: MILLER *enters, carrying basket of pumpernickel bread.*

MILLER: Where could the King be? Ah . . . here comes someone now. (HUNTER *enters with gun and some rabbits.*) Oh — it's only a hunter. (*To* HUNTER) Good day, sir. Why have *you* come to see the King?

HUNTER: To give him a present, Miller. And why are you here?

MILLER: I also have a gift for the King. I see you have some rabbits. Did you catch them yourself?

HUNTER: Yes. I am the finest hunter in the land.

MILLER: Oh, you are, are you?

HUNTER: Yes. I can catch as many as five hundred rabbits in one day. These are only a few I caught this morning.

35

MILLER: My, that is a lot of rabbits. But that doesn't compare to the amount of flour I mill in one day. Milling 500 sacks of flour is but a start for me. See here! (*Holds out basket*) I have brought a delicious loaf of bread made from my wheat.

HUNTER: Let me have a slice.

MILLER: Oh, no! I have brought this bread for the King. (*He exits.*)

HUNTER: Humph! Five hundred sacks of flour in one day. . . . Impossible! These rabbits are getting heavy. I do wish the King would appear so that I can give them to him. I want him to appoint me Royal Hunter for the castle. (KING enters.) Good day, Your Majesty. (*He bows deeply.*)

KING: Good day, Hunter. You wish to see me?

HUNTER: I wish to present the rabbits that I caught for you. (*Gives rabbits to* KING)

KING: Why, thank you! There are many rabbits here. You must be a good hunter.

HUNTER: Yes, I am. I can offer you anything in the woods — a deer, a unicorn, or perhaps a questing beast. Just name it and I will hunt it down. I can also find any lost pet animals for you, because I know the forest so well.

KING: I hope you are not lying, for there has been too much bragging and too much fibbing recently. You may stay on and be Royal Hunter for the castle, but you must prove your trustworthiness.

HUNTER: Oh, thank you, Your Majesty. (*He exits.*)

KING: Unicorn! Questing beast! Really! Some people do carry on so. I must do something about all this falsehood going about. Such fabrications. But what? Someone must pay the penalty and serve as an example. (MILLER enters.)

MILLER: Your Majesty (*Bows*) — Your Majesty (*Bows*) — Your Majesty (*Bows*) —

KING: Yes, Miller. May I help you?

MILLER: I, your humble servant, have come to present to you this loaf of pumpernickel bread. I have milled the flour, and my daughter, Sarah, has baked it especially for you.

KING (*Taking basket*): Thank you, good Miller. (*Tastes bread*) Hm-m-m. This is delicious. I do wish I had a wife who could bake like this. And one that could spin cloth, for my weavers are all so clumsy. I would make her my queen.

MILLER: Oh, my daughter is very clever. Not only can she bake, but she can spin straw into gold.

KING: Did you say your daughter could spin straw into gold?

MILLER (*To audience*): I think I said the wrong thing. (*To* KING) Ah . . . yes!

KING: If your daughter can spin straw into gold as well as she can bake pumpernickel bread, I will marry her. But if she cannot, I will throw you into my dungeons to punish you for lying.

MILLER: But, Your Majesty . . .

KING: Be off with you. Bring your daughter here tomorrow.

MILLER: Good day, Your Majesty. Good day! (*To himself*) Oh, what did I say? (*Exits*)

KING: A girl that spins straw into gold? We shall see. We shall see. (*Curtain*)

*　　*　　*　　*　　*

SCENE 2

SETTING: *The royal treasury. There is a spinning wheel at one side of stage, with pile of straw beside it.*

AT RISE: MILLER *enters with* SARAH, *his daughter.*

SARAH: But, Papa, I can't spin straw into gold. No one can.

MILLER: If you do, you will be Queen. You must try, dear. I will be sent to the dungeons if you don't.

SARAH: I will try, Papa.

MILLER: The King is coming. I had better leave you. Do the best you can. Goodbye, dear.

SARAH: Goodbye, Papa. (MILLER *exits.*) What will I say? What will I do? I must save poor Papa. I'm sure he must have meant well. (KING *enters.*)

KING: Good day, pretty child. You must be Sarah, the Miller's daughter.

SARAH: Good day, Your Majesty. Yes, I am Sarah.

KING: Thank you for the delicious bread you baked for me yesterday.

SARAH: For your pleasure, Your Majesty.

KING: Your father tells me you can spin.

SARAH: Yes, I can spin.

KING: He tells me you can spin straw into gold. You have been brought here to prove that what your father claims is true. (*Points to straw*) Here is a bundle of straw. Spin this into gold.

SARAH: But, Your Majesty . . .

KING: Yes? Did you wish to tell me something?

SARAH: Ah . . . no, sir.

KING: I will leave you now, but I will be back soon. If you have accomplished the deed when I return, you will be my wife and Queen. If you have not, I'm afraid your father will be thrown into my dungeons for fibbing. (*He exits.*)

SARAH: What shall I do? I'll try. (SARAH *begins to spin.*) Just put the straw to the spinning wheel. . . . (*Tries again*) Oh, dear. Nothing happens. Poor Papa! What will I do? (*She breaks down and cries.*) Boo-hoo. (RUMPELSTILTSKIN *enters.*)

RUMPELSTILTSKIN: Good day, girl.

SARAH (*Surprised*): Oh! Who are you?

RUMPELSTILTSKIN: Never mind who I am. I know who you are and I know you have a problem.

SARAH: Yes. I must spin —

RUMPELSTILTSKIN: Straw into gold. I know all about it. And your father will suffer if you do not. Tsk, tsk! What some people get themselves into. Hm-m-m. Perhaps I can help you.

SARAH: Can you? But how? No one can spin straw into gold!

RUMPELSTILTSKIN: *I* can. But you must give me something precious for my services.

SARAH: I have so little. Now, what can I give you? Would you take my necklace?

RUMPELSTILTSKIN: Well — yes! It is a pretty thing. I can wrap it about my waist.

SARAH (*Taking off necklace*): Here it is. Take it. (*He takes necklace.*)

RUMPELSTILTSKIN: Now I'll get to work. Close your eyes and no peeking. (*She covers her face with her hands, and he spins.*)

>Whirl, whirl, here we go,
>Just so fast and not too slow.
>All this gold, see it glow.

(*Draws length of golden cord from straw.*) You can look now.

SARAH (*Uncovering her eyes and seeing gold*): Oh, how wonderful! You did do it! My papa is safe now. Thank you so much, Mr. — what did you say your name was?

RUMPELSTILTSKIN: I didn't say. (*Laughs*) Goodbye. (*Disappears*)

SARAH: What a funny little man. He must be a magician.

KING (*From offstage*): Sarah! Have you finished spinning? May I come in?

SARAH: Come in, Your Majesty. (KING *enters.*)

KING: Why, you *have* turned the straw into gold! There is enough to buy you a beautiful wedding dress — for we are to be married.

SARAH: And Papa won't be thrown into the dungeons?

KING: That's right. He will be Royal Miller instead.

SARAH (*Bowing*): Thank you, Your Majesty.

KING: But I wonder . . . would you spin some more straw, so that we could have a wonderful wedding feast for the entire court? (*Brings out straw*) Here is more straw. We must have a proper party.

SARAH: I could bake some more pumpernickel bread.

KING: It was delicious, but we must have cookies, cake, ice cream and spaghetti. Now get to work. I'll be right back. (*Exits*)

SARAH: Oh, dear! (*Beginning to cry*) Now what will I do? I do wish that little man would come back.

RUMPELSTILTSKIN (*Entering*): Here I am. I heard your call. What's wrong this time?

SARAH: The King has brought more straw — much more — so that we can have enough gold for a wedding feast.

RUMPELSTILTSKIN: And you want me to spin this straw into gold, too? (*She nods.*) What do you have to give me this time?

SARAH: Now, let me see . . . (*Looks about, then at her hand*) All I have left of value is this ring my mother gave to me.

RUMPELSTILTSKIN: That will do. Give it to me! (*She gives ring to him.*) Now turn around and hide your eyes. (*He spins*)

> Spin, spin, thick and thin,
> To help the maiden and her kin,
> Someday Sarah the King will win.

(*Draws out more gold from straw.*) You can look now!

SARAH: Wonderful! Thank you again. I will always be grateful to you.

RUMPELSTILTSKIN: Yes, my dear, you will be grateful! (*Laughs and exits.*)

SARAH: It's amazing how he does it. I just hope that was the last time I need to call him. I have nothing left to give him. (KING *enters.*)

KING: Well, my dear, that didn't take you long. We shall have a magnificent feast with this much gold. But there is still one thing lacking, and that is a new wedding coach for us. I'm sure you won't mind spinning a bit more straw. Here is a pile that should only take you a moment. (*He brings in large bundle of straw.*) Call me when you are done. (*He exits.*)

SARAH: Oh, my! Now what shall I do? (RUMPELSTILTSKIN *appears.*)

RUMPELSTILTSKIN: Well, here we are again. Still in trouble, eh?

SARAH: This is the last time, little man. Please help me again.

RUMPELSTILTSKIN: What do you have to offer this time?

SARAH: I've given you all my precious possessions. Surely you will still help me. It takes you so little time.

RUMPELSTILTSKIN: You must pay for know-how, my dear. If you have nothing to offer, I will leave. Goodbye!

SARAH: Wait! There must be something — (*Searches*) What will I do? (*Weeps*)

RUMPELSTILTSKIN: Maybe we can figure something out. Now, let's see. You are going to marry the King?

SARAH: Yes . . .

RUMPELSTILTSKIN: And be Queen?

SARAH: Yes . . .

RUMPELSTILTSKIN: And after a year or so have a little child?

SARAH: Oh, I hope so!

RUMPELSTILTSKIN: Fine! Then as payment for the gold you must promise to give me your first-born child.

SARAH: Oh, no! I beg of you. Take anything else — my crown, my jewels, my —

RUMPELSTILTSKIN: Your first child — nothing more or less. Come now. I'm in a hurry. Your answer?

SARAH: All right. I agree. (*She covers her face and he spins.*)

RUMPELSTILTSKIN:

> Roll, roll, gold so fine,
> Sarah's goodness is a sign
> That her first child will be mine.

(*Draws very long length of golden cord from straw, then cackles wickedly and exits*)

SARAH (*Uncovering her eyes*): My first child — to be taken from me. Oh, no! I must protect my baby! (KING *enters.*)

KING: Sarah! (*Sees gold*) Why, this is more gold than I ever expected. We have enough for a new castle. I don't want to be greedy, so I promise you will never have to spin gold again. And we will be so happy . . .

SARAH: Yes (*Sadly*) . . . so happy . . . (*They exit. Curtain.*)

*   *   *   *   *

SCENE 3

SETTING: *Nursery. Cradle, with canopy of rich-looking cloth over it, is at center.*

AT RISE: SARAH, *now in royal robe and crown, holds* BABY. KING *enters.*

KING: Oh, there you are, my dear Queen Sarah . . . and my new little baby girl. She's just as pretty as her mother. I am going to arrange a christening party for her. Take care of our little princess, Sarah. We wouldn't want anything to happen to her. (KING *exits.*)

SARAH: My sweet little girl. We are so lucky to have you.
(BABY *coos.*) Go to sleep. (*Sings*)
> My sweet little dear,
> I'll sing you to sleep,
> With all our love, for you to keep.
> Here's all we can give you.
> What more can I say?

(RUMPELSTILTSKIN *enters.*)

RUMPELSTILTSKIN: Now I've come to take her away. (*Laughs*)

SARAH: You've come back! Leave this castle at once!

RUMPELSTILTSKIN: I've come for my payment. Have you forgotten? Give me the child!

SARAH: Oh, no. Not my baby. Take anything — there's gold, my crown, jewels, anything — but don't take my baby!

RUMPELSTILTSKIN: I don't want your jewels. I am lonesome in the woods and I want someone to play with. I must have the child.

SARAH: You are cruel and mean! She is a princess, and she should stay here with us. (SARAH *cries and* BABY *cries.*)

RUMPELSTILTSKIN: Oh, I hate to see women cry! Don't cry. I ... well ... I'll give you another chance.

SARAH: Oh, would you? Please?

RUMPELSTILTSKIN: If you can guess my name within twenty-four hours, you can keep the child, and I won't bother you again. If not, you must give me your crown, your jewels, and all the gold in the castle ... and the baby as well.

SARAH: Yes — yes, little man! Is your name Paul? Is it Peter? Is it —

RUMPELSTILTSKIN (*Laughing*): Ha-ha! Remember, twenty-four hours and then the little princess will be mine. (*Laughs*) Ha-ha! (*Exits*)

SARAH: His name? Surely it won't be so difficult to find out his name. I know. I'll call the Hunter. Perhaps he can find out. (*Calls*) Hunter! (HUNTER *enters.*)

HUNTER: Did you call, O Queen?

SARAH: There was a little man here, just a moment ago. I must know his name, or he will take the baby.

HUNTER: Take the baby? Oh, no!

SARAH: Search the land — through the woods, the hills and mountains, the forest. We have but twenty-four hours. We *must* know his name.

HUNTER: What did he look like?

SARAH: He is very short and has a big bushy beard. He wears a stocking cap and pointed shoes. He couldn't be far from the castle yet — see if you can catch him.

HUNTER: Yes, Your Majesty. I'll hurry. (*Exits*)

SARAH (*Calling*): Yes, do. Hurry! (*Curtain*)

*   *   *   *   *

SCENE 4

SETTING: *The woods. This scene may be played before curtain.*

AT RISE: RUMPELSTILTSKIN *is skipping around stage. He does not see* HUNTER, *who is hiding behind trees, peering out, then ducking as* RUMPELSTILTSKIN *comes near.*

RUMPELSTILTSKIN (*Singing*):

> It won't be long, if my luck is good,
> I'll have a playmate in the wood.
> The Queen will help me win the game—
> She can't guess Rumpelstiltskin is my name.

(*Laughs*) A playmate! Ha-ha! A princess! (*Shouts*) Rumpelstiltskin—oops! Sh-h-h! (*Softly*) Rumpelstiltskin is my name. (*To audience*) Now, don't you tell anyone! (*Laughs and exits.* HUNTER *comes out of hiding.*)

HUNTER: So that's it! His name is Rumpelstiltskin! (*Runs off. Curtain.*)

*   *   *   *   *

SCENE 5

SETTING: *Nursery. Same as Scene 3.*
AT RISE: SARAH, *holding* BABY, *is pacing up and down.*

SARAH: Oh, where is the Hunter? The time is almost up. The little man will be here soon. Oh, dear. ... (HUNTER *enters.*)
HUNTER: Here I am, Your Majesty. (*Bows*)
SARAH: Did you find him?
HUNTER: I hunted the woods over. I hunted and searched and hunted and —
SARAH: Did you find him? Get on with it!
HUNTER: I came to a dark part of the forest where I had never been before, and there he was. I hid behind a tree and watched as he danced about and sang a little song. He said his name was ... ah ... Oh, dear. I forgot!
SARAH: Oh, no!
HUNTER (*To audience*): What was his name? (*Audience calls "Rumpelstiltskin."*) Yes, that's right. Rumpelstiltskin. Thank you ever so much.
SARAH: Rumpel— What did you say?
HUNTER: Rumpelstiltskin!
SARAH: Rumpelstiltskin! What an odd name. Thank you so much, Hunter.
HUNTER: You're welcome.
SARAH: Now you had better go. He will soon be here.
HUNTER: Yes, Your Majesty. Good day. (*He exits.*)
SARAH: Rumpelstiltskin — what a long, long name for such a little, little man! I will not forget this name. Never. (RUMPELSTILTSKIN *enters.*)

RUMPELSTILTSKIN: I've come for the child. Is she ready?

SARAH: I still have five minutes. I want my chance to guess your name.

RUMPELSTILTSKIN: You'll never guess. Give me the baby — quickly!

SARAH: No. I have five minutes. Is your name Oswald?

RUMPELSTILTSKIN: No! No! Give me the baby.

SARAH: Is it Thomas or Gerald or Geronimo?

RUMPELSTILTSKIN: No! No! Give me the baby, right away!

SARAH: Could it possibly be *Rumpelstiltskin?*

RUMPELSTILTSKIN: I want the — what? *What did you say?*

SARAH: I said, is your name Rumpelstiltskin?

RUMPELSTILTSKIN: How did you guess? Who told you? You found out! I'm so angry I could stamp my foot. (*Stamps foot*) I'm *so* angry! (*Stamps*) *So* angry! (*Stamps again*) *Angry!* (*Stamps so hard that he falls through floor and disappears, crying out*) Ah-h-h-h-h!

SARAH (*Crossing to where he disappeared*): My! He certainly did make a big hole in my new parquet floor. Poor little man. (KING *enters quickly.*)

KING: Sarah! Did I hear someone shouting? (*Sees hole*) And how did that hole get in the floor?

SARAH: I had a contest with a little man, and I'm afraid he lost.

KING: I guess he *is* lost.

SARAH: A little man tried to take our baby, and the earth just opened up and swallowed him.

KING: He must be clear to China by now. But our princess?

SARAH: She is just fine.

KING: But what was the man's name?

SARAH: Rumpelstiltskin.

KING (*Looking into hole*): Well, goodbye, Rumpelstiltskin. (*To audience*) And goodbye, everyone.

QUEEN (*To audience*): Goodbye! (*Bows, as curtains close*)

THE END

Production Notes

RUMPELSTILTSKIN

Number of Puppets: 7 puppets or marionettes.

Playing Time: 20 minutes.

Description of Puppets: Rumpelstiltskin is very short, with a beard, stocking cap and pointed elf's shoes. Hunter is dressed in green. King wears royal robes and crown. There should be two Sarah puppets, the first in a plain dress and apron, the second in royal robes, with a crown. Miller is dressed like a peasant.

Properties: Toy, basket of dark bread, toy rabbits and small rifle, toy spinning wheel, straw, golden cords.

Setting: For Scenes 1, 2, 3 and 5, the set should be a room in the palace with stone walls. Replace throne, used in Scene 1, with spinning wheel in Scene 2 and cradle in Scenes 3 and 5. Banners and tapestry may be changed also, if desired. Scene 4, the woods, may be played before curtain, or a painted backdrop of trees may be placed in front of palace set. In Scene 5, if puppets are used, Rumpelstiltskin falls behind stage at end. If using marionettes for this scene, build a raised section of the floor, through which he falls. In Scene 2, golden cord can be beneath stage and pulled up through a small hole in floor.

Lighting: No special effects.

KING MIDAS AND THE GOLDEN TOUCH

Characters

NARRATOR
KING MIDAS
MARIGOLD, *his daughter*
JOHANNA, *her nurse*
JONATHAN, *a manservant*
ORO, *the Spirit of Gold*
GOLDIE, *the cat*

SCENE 1

SETTING: *King Midas's throne room, with a beautiful garden alive with flowers at one side. The sun is shining.*
AT RISE: KING MIDAS *and* JONATHAN *enter.*

NARRATOR: There once lived a king called Midas. He had more gold than any other king or rich man anywhere in the world, yet King Midas was not content. He always wished for more and more gold.
MIDAS: I don't want to think about the country's problems. I don't have time. I have to find new ways to get gold.
JONATHAN: But there are papers to sign. And your fields need planting. We must buy seeds for your farmers to sow.
MIDAS: But that costs money. I have no gold to spare.
JONATHAN: Your people are waiting in the hall to speak to you. Some have been waiting for many days. There are problems to be solved.
MIDAS: Well, they will just have to wait. It's time to count my gold.

(*Sings to the tune of "Three Blind Mice"*)
> Duties tend — know I should.
> What I like — if I could
> Is counting gold and by the score.
> Any other work is a bore,
> For gold is what I do adore.
> I love gold!

(*He does a little dance.*)
> Better none — than yellow gold.
> None so rare — so I'm told.
> So please excuse me if I stray
> From my chores this very day.
> Listen to what I have to say —
> I love gold!

JONATHAN: But, Your Majesty . . .

MARIGOLD (*Entering with her cat,* GOLDIE): Good morning, Daddy.

MIDAS: Good morning, Marigold. Isn't she the sweetest child you've ever seen, Jonathan?

JONATHAN: Yes, she certainly is, King Midas.

MIDAS: I'm so lucky to have such a good little girl. (MARIGOLD *is playing with* GOLDIE) Come over to me, my sweet, and give Papa a kiss.

MARIGOLD (*Coming over*): For the dearest Daddy in the world. (*Kisses him*)

MIDAS: That's my girl.

MARIGOLD: Look at Goldie, Papa. See how she plays. (GOLDIE *romps around*)

MIDAS: Yes, she is a good companion, isn't she?

MARIGOLD: But I'd rather you played with me, Papa. Come to the garden and see my pretty flowers. They are all the colors of the rainbow. Aren't they beautiful? (*Sings to the tune of "London Bridge Is Falling Down"*)

Look, my flowers, see how nice,
Smell them too, once or twice,
Smell their fragrance, to entice
My dear Daddy.
Marigold and roses, too,
Daffodils, violets blue,
Come and see my daisy too —
My dear Daddy.

MIDAS: Not now, dear. I have to go with Jonathan to the treasure room and count gold.

MARIGOLD: But you just counted your gold yesterday morning. It's surely still there.

MIDAS: Now, Marigold, your father knows best. Run along and play with Goldie.

MARIGOLD (*Disappointed*): Yes, Father. Come along, Goldie. Let's play in the garden. (MARIGOLD *and* GOLDIE *exit into garden.*)

MIDAS: Jonathan, come along to the treasure room.

JONATHAN: Yes, Your Majesty. (*They exit. Curtain*)

*   *   *   *   *

SCENE 2

SETTING: *The treasure room, dark and foreboding. Only one shaft of light enters room, at center. There is a candlestick at one side. Room is filled with chests and bags of gold.*

AT RISE: MIDAS *and* JONATHAN *enter.*

MIDAS: Now, where did we leave off? Oh, yes, with this bag. Do you have the accounting book, Jonathan?

JONATHAN: Yes, Your Majesty. Call out the numbers and I'll mark them off. (*Opens book*)

MIDAS: Good idea! Now, let's see. (*Counting*) Two million, twenty-five . . .

JONATHAN: Two million, twenty-five. Yes.

MIDAS: Two million, twenty-six. Two million, twenty-seven. Two million, twenty-eight!

JONATHAN: Got it, Your Majesty. Wait! I must go and get another candle. I'll be right back. (*He exits.*)

MIDAS: All this gold. They say I am the richest man in the world, but that can't be right. Surely there must be some other way to get more gold. . . . Tax the people? No, that wouldn't be fair. I'm fond of my subjects and they like me. Wage war on a nearby country and take their gold? No, I'm a gentle person and wouldn't want to do that. If there were just some way . . . Hm-m-m. I just love to touch all my beautiful gold. Better than any other thing in the world, except my beautiful, sweet daughter, Marigold. Touch . . . touch . . . that's it. I wish I had the Golden Touch. I wish . . . I wish that whatever I touch would turn to gold. (*There is a mysterious sound of bells and a golden figure,* ORO, *comes from the beam of light.*) What's this? A golden man . . . in that shaft of light. Who are you?

ORO (*Chanting*):

> Oro is my name, the Spirit of Gold.
> I can also bring you riches untold.
> I can grant the wish you want so much —
> That is, if you want the golden touch.
>
> Then now, think twice before you say
> What is on your mind. It's best to weigh
> What you wish to have. Just let me know
> And I promise that I'll make it so.

MIDAS: The Golden Touch. Oh, yes! How wonderful. What must I do?

ORO: Just wait until the sun rises tomorrow morning and

then your wish will come true. Goodbye, King Midas. And I hope you will be happy with your new power.

MIDAS: Thank you, Oro, Spirit of Gold. Thank you. How wonderful! The Golden Touch! (ORO *exits.*) Oh! He is gone!

JONATHAN (*Offstage*): Your Majesty . . .

MIDAS: I'd better not tell anyone. I'm sure they wouldn't believe me anyway. I'll just wait until it happens. (*He snickers.*)

JONATHAN (*Entering*): Did I hear you talking to someone?

MIDAS: Me? Talking to someone? (*Laughs*) No, no. Don't be silly. I was just talking . . . er . . . counting to myself.

JONATHAN: Shall we get back to the accounts?

MIDAS: No, let's take the rest of the day off. Perhaps I'll see my subjects now. And here is some gold to buy seed for the farmers to plant. (*Hands* JONATHAN *a bag of gold*) I feel quite generous today. (*He laughs as they exit. Curtain*)

*   *   *   *   *

SCENE 3

TIME: *The next day, before dawn.*
SETTING: *The same as Scene 1.*
AT RISE: MIDAS *runs in.*

MIDAS: Oh, my. Today is the day! Where is Jonathan? Where is Johanna? Let's get things started today. (*He pulls cord and sound of bell is heard.* JOHANNA *runs in.*)

JOHANNA: Your Majesty. Up so early? Usually you sleep until noon.

MIDAS: Well, I . . .

JONATHAN (*Running in*): King Midas? Up so early? Usually you . . .

MIDAS: Sleep till noon. Yes, I know, but today is a special day.

JONATHAN: It is? Is it your birthday?

MIDAS: No. . . . (*Laughs*)

JOHANNA: Is it the princess's birthday?

MIDAS: No, but watch. (*He touches curtains and nothing happens.*)

JOHANNA: Would you like the curtains down, Your Majesty?

MIDAS: What happened? Why aren't they gold?

JOHANNA: I can change them to gold-colored ones, Your Majesty.

MIDAS: No, you don't understand.

JONATHAN: We will lower them when the sun rises.

MIDAS: When the sun rises . . . that's it. The sun isn't up yet.

JOHANNA: But the sun is just rising now. See what a pretty day it will be!

MARIGOLD (*Entering*): Good morning, Papa. Come out into the garden and play with me.

MIDAS: Another time, dear. Johanna, take Marigold for a walk. Today is my special day.

MARIGOLD: But Papa. You promised.

JOHANNA: Come along, child. Your father is busy.

MARIGOLD: Yes, Johanna. Perhaps we can pick some of my beautiful flowers. I'm so happy when I'm in the garden. Goodbye, Papa.

MIDAS: Goodbye, dear. Have a good time. (MARIGOLD *and* JOHANNA *exit.*) Ah, now! Now for the wonderful surprise. The sun has risen — now look! (*He touches curtains and they turn to gold. See Production Notes for changing objects to gold.*) Ha-ha!

JONATHAN: Amazing. How did you do that?

MIDAS: Now watch this. (*He touches his throne and it turns to gold. He laughs.*) Isn't this wonderful?

JONATHAN: Well, I say . . .

MIDAS: I have the Golden Touch! Whatever I touch turns to gold. Don't you think I'm lucky?

JONATHAN: I guess so, Your Majesty. But all that counting! We will never finish this way. We will have to build a new treasury to hold all this.

MIDAS (*Laughing*): Everything will be so beautiful. Solid gold. But I'm so hungry. Have you my breakfast?

JONATHAN: Right here. (*He gets a tray that holds bread and eggs.*)

MIDAS: Hm-m-m. Looks delicious. I'm famished. I haven't had anything to eat since supper last night. Let's see! Think I'll open my egg first. It looks so good and I love eggs. (*He touches egg and it turns to gold.*) Oh! My egg is solid gold. Oh, dear! I'll try a piece of bread. (*It turns to gold*) Oh, no!

JONATHAN: What is wrong?

MIDAS: My food. My food turns to gold. I'll have to be fed. That's ridiculous!

JONATHAN: Yes, Your Majesty.

MIDAS: What?

JONATHAN: How wonderful to have the Golden Touch.

MIDAS: Yes, it . . . is, isn't it? Marigold will be so pleased. I know, I'll touch all her flowers so they will be presents of solid gold.

JONATHAN: But, Your Majesty . . . (MIDAS *goes to garden and touches flowers. They turn to gold.*)

MIDAS: Look! Look! Aren't they beautiful now? Come, Jonathan. Let's see what else we can turn to gold.

JONATHAN: Yes, King Midas. (*They exit, and* MARIGOLD *and* JOHANNA *enter.*)

MARIGOLD: Such a pretty day. Thank you, Johanna, for taking me for my walk.

JOHANNA: Don't you think you should take a nap, dear Marigold?

MARIGOLD: In a minute. I just want to see and smell my pretty flowers again. (*She turns and sees them.*) Oh, no! My pretty flowers. What happened to them? They are all hard and brittle. And they have lost their beautiful perfume. (*She cries.*)

MIDAS (*Entering*): What's wrong, dear sweet daughter? Why do you cry so? Johanna, get Marigold a handkerchief for her tears.

JOHANNA: Yes, Your Majesty. (*She exits.*)

MARIGOLD: My pretty flowers. They've all died and have turned to stone. (*Cries*)

MIDAS: Stone? No, dear ... that's gold. Solid gold!

MARIGOLD: But I loved them as they were. Oh, what will I do without my rainbow garden? (*She cries harder.*)

MIDAS: Now, don't cry. I can't bear to see you cry. Here ... come to Papa and let me kiss your tears away. (*He kisses her and she turns to golden statue.*) Marigold! Marigold ... what have I done? What *have* I done? (*Calls*) Oro! Spirit of Gold ... come back!

ORO (*Appearing*): King Midas, is something wrong? How do you like your Golden Touch?

MIDAS: Please, please, save my little girl. I don't want the Golden Touch. Take it away. Give me back my child.

ORO: Greed is a misery. Count your blessings for what you already have. Never again will you have the Golden Touch. Share your great wealth with your people.

MIDAS: Anything. ... Only return Marigold to me.

ORO: Soon a magical snow will fall. Place Marigold among her flowers. Then promise that never again will you want more than your fair share on this earth. Be kind to your subjects and be happy with what you have.

MIDAS: Yes, oh, yes. Thank you, Oro, Spirit of Gold. I swear! I have learned my lesson. (*It starts to snow. See Production Notes.*)

ORO: Look! The snow is here. Quickly!

MIDAS: Oh, yes! (MIDAS *picks up statue of his daughter and puts it among the flowers.*)

ORO: Goodbye, King Midas.

MIDAS: Goodbye . . . and thank you again. (ORO *exits. The snow continues to fall. The flowers change back.*) Look! Marigold's flowers are back. Please bring my daughter back to me! Never again will I be greedy. I promise I will be thoughtful of others. My poor little girl! (*He puts his face in his hands. Statue turns to* MARIGOLD. *Snow stops.*)

MARIGOLD: Look, Papa! My flowers are real again. How good they smell.

MIDAS (*Looking up*): Marigold, you are back. (*He runs to her.*)

MARIGOLD: My garden is more beautiful than ever. And the soft snow makes the flowers fresh and pretty. (JONATHAN *and* JOHANNA *enter.*)

MIDAS: Look, everyone. Marigold is back!

JOHANNA: Back from our walk? But Your Majesty, we weren't gone long.

JONATHAN: The walk has brought fresh beauty to little Marigold.

MIDAS: Jonathan, get 100 bags of gold to give to my people.

JONATHAN: What did you say, King Midas?

MIDAS: You heard me. One hundred bags of gold. Hurry now . . .

JONATHAN: Yes, Your Majesty. (*He exits.*)

MIDAS: Johanna, dress Marigold in her best, for today we visit our people. It is time to share! It is time for giving! It is time for love! (MIDAS *embraces* MARIGOLD *and she then runs off with* JOHANNA. MIDAS *goes into the garden among the flowers. Curtain.*)

THE END

Production Notes

KING MIDAS AND THE GOLDEN TOUCH

Number of Puppets: 6 hand or rod puppets or marionettes.
Characters: 1 male or female for Narrator.
Playing Time: 15 minutes.
Description of Puppets: King Midas is kindly and gray-haired. Marigold is a little girl with blonde hair. Jonathan and Johanna are middle-aged and kindly. The cat is yellow. Oro can be an old elf or a handsome youth dressed in gold with yellow hair. The play can take place at any time, but Grecian costumes would be nice. Costume or fairy-tale books will give you ideas.
Properties: Book, bags of gold, tray with bread and eggs.
Setting: Scenes 1 and 3: throne room and flower garden. There is a throne at one side. On wall are curtained window and bell cord. Scene 2: treasure room, with bags of gold and candlestick.
Lighting: Scene 1 is bright and sunny, Scene 2 is dark with only a single shaft of light from above, and Scene 3 is dim at beginning and brightens.
Sound: Sound of bells when Oro enters.
Special Effects: For turning objects into gold: either use the flip-down prop that covers the original with a golden version, or quickly exchange original object with a golden one. Use a turn-about throne, golden on one side. The curtains that turn to gold can be any color and, when pulled down, have top section of gold. Marigold, when turned to gold, is a golden statue version of the puppet. The flowers can be painted with a flip-down version in gold or else exchanged quickly with another identical set painted gold.

58

To make it snow, make a trough of muslin and two pieces of wood and cut slits diagonally all along the muslin. Suspend this from the top of your stage and fill with artificial snow made of bits of plastic or white paper. When jiggled from below by an attached cord, the trough will allow the snow to fall softly on the scene at the back of the stage. Oro should always appear from above or below, never from the side of the stage.

SLEEPING BEAUTY

Characters

NARRATOR
QUEEN
KING
HEDGEHOG
BRIAR ROSE
FAIRY VIOLET
FAIRY RUBY
FAIRY GOLDEN
FAIRY GRUNDELL
PRINCE
BLACK CAT
DRAGON

SCENE 1

BEFORE RISE: NARRATOR *comes out and addresses audience.*

NARRATOR: Once upon a time, there lived a King and Queen in their happy kingdom. They were good and kind to their subjects and were well loved by all. There was only one thing missing from their happy lives — they didn't have any children.... (*Exits as curtains open*)

*   *   *

SETTING: *The castle garden.*
AT RISE: KING *and* QUEEN *enter.*

61

KING: It's such a nice day, my dear. Why do you look so glum?

QUEEN: Don't mind me, good husband. We've been married many years and still we do not have a sweet child to play with.

KING: Life has been good to us otherwise. Perhaps one day we will have an heir to inherit our kingdom and brighten our days.

QUEEN: I do hope so.

KING: I must leave you to attend to business of the court. Enjoy the garden, my dear.

QUEEN: Until later, dear husband. (*He exits.*) I'm sure he wants a baby too — a little one to play by our side.

HEDGEHOG (*Entering*): Hello, there.

QUEEN: It's a little hedgehog.

HEDGEHOG: I could not help but hear what you said, my Queen. I live here in your garden. Your wish will come true.

QUEEN: And do you know what the wish of my heart is?

HEDGEHOG: It is to have a little child of your own.

QUEEN: That is true — a beautiful little baby.

HEDGEHOG: You must wait one year and then you will have a baby girl.

QUEEN: Thank you for your wonderful news, Master Hedgehog.

HEDGEHOG: Goodbye, my Queen . . . and good luck.

QUEEN: Goodbye, little friend. (HEDGEHOG *exits.*) Husband! Husband! Listen!

KING (*Entering*): What is it? Is anything wrong?

QUEEN: Wrong? No — a good omen. A hedgehog just told me we are to have a baby.

KING: A hedgehog? (*Comforting her*) Yes, dear . . . yes, dear. It's best you come in now, out of the sun.

QUEEN: A baby — just for us. (*They exit. Curtain*)

* * * * *

SCENE 2

BEFORE RISE: NARRATOR *addresses audience.*

NARRATOR: The Hedgehog's words came true. The Queen had a little girl and she was named Briar Rose for the beautiful briar roses that grew row by row in the garden. On her christening day the King and Queen gave a party and invited all but one of the thirteen fairies in the kingdom. (*Exits. Curtains open.*)

* * *

SETTING: *The throne room.*

AT RISE: FAIRY VIOLET, FAIRY RUBY *and* FAIRY GOLDEN *are at left.* KING *and* QUEEN *stand near baby's crib.*

KING: It is so good to have you all here at the christening of our little girl. Welcome! Welcome!

QUEEN: Isn't she a sweet baby? We are so proud. Our first child, you know. A hedgehog once told me . . .

KING (*Interrupting* QUEEN): Please continue with your gifts, good fairies.

FAIRIES (*Singing to tune of "London Bridge Is Falling Down"*):

> Join us here in wishes true.
> Place them here, they are due.
> Take them all, we love her, too,
> Our sweet Princess.
> Take them all and don't despair,
> Give them out with loving care.

> Thoughtful gifts, you'll see, so rare,
> For our Princess.

QUEEN: Lovely ... lovely ...

FAIRY VIOLET: Nine of our sisters have presented their gifts to the new princess, My Queen. There are but three of us left. My gift to the child is that she be beautiful and kind all her life.

QUEEN: Thank you, Fairy Violet. We hope that she will be.

FAIRY VIOLET: Goodbye, my friends. Now I must go prepare the flowers for spring.

QUEEN: Have a pretty spring!

ALL: Goodbye. (*She exits.*)

FAIRY RUBY (*To* FAIRY GOLDEN): Did you notice that Fairy Grundell wasn't invited? If she finds out about the party she will be furious.

FAIRY GOLDEN: I understand there were only twelve golden plates for our supper. That must be the reason. Nearly all twelve of us have left. Just you and I are here to protect the sweet little child. I will look out for Fairy Grundell. She may be on the castle grounds. (*She exits.*)

FAIRY RUBY: And as next to the last good fairy, I, Fairy Ruby, present Princess Briar Rose with the gift of dance. (FAIRY RUBY *dances and all applaud.*)

KING: Thank you, dear Fairy Ruby. (*She exits.*)

FAIRY GRUNDELL (*Offstage*): Stand aside! Stand aside, or I'll turn you into a lizard! (*She enters.*) So-o-o — it's true. Everyone was invited but me. Ah-h-h ... to celebrate a new princess. And gifts — a ball, a crown, good tidings and wishes. I think I should give a gift, too. Let me see, what shall it be?

KING: I don't think we need any gifts from you, Fairy Grundell.

FAIRY GRUNDELL: But a gift she shall receive. When Princess Briar Rose reaches the age of sixteen she shall prick her finger on a spindle and die. (*She laughs evilly.*)

ALL (*Ad lib*): No! You can't do that!

KING: Grundell, you evil fairy. You are to leave this kingdom and never return again. Go!

FAIRY GRUNDELL: That will not save her. Remember, when she is sixteen . . . (*Laughing, she exits.*)

QUEEN (*Crying*): Oh, husband. What shall we do? My poor baby.

HEDGEHOG (*Entering*): My King and Queen. Do not lose heart. Listen . . .

QUEEN: There's my little hedgehog.

KING: How did he get in here?

QUEEN: You once told me of my baby's birth. Do you have more good news?

HEDGEHOG: You have forgotten Fairy Golden. She can help to save Princess Briar Rose.

FAIRY GOLDEN (*Entering*): I cannot remove the curse, but I have not given my gift yet. (*Crossing to baby's crib*) Sweet Briar Rose, should Fairy Grundell's spell fall on you, I pledge you will not die, but will sleep one hundred years until a handsome prince kisses you. Then you and all in the castle will awake.

QUEEN: Dear Fairy Golden, we are eternally grateful to you.

KING: And to the hedgehog, as well.

HEDGEHOG: My good wishes too. I will be nearby. (HEDGEHOG *exits.*)

FAIRY GOLDEN: Goodbye for now.

ALL: Goodbye. (FAIRY GOLDEN *exits. Curtain.*)

*   *   *   *   *

SCENE 3

BEFORE RISE: NARRATOR *addresses audience.*

NARRATOR: The King, fearing for Briar Rose's safety, had all spinning wheels, shuttles and bobbins in the palace and nearby towns destroyed. Yarns and threads had to be brought in from other cities and boroughs for clothes and soft goods. Meanwhile, Briar Rose grew into a charming, beautiful, kind girl. (*Exits. Curtains open.*)

*   *   *

SETTING: *Same as Scene 1, sixteen years later.*
AT RISE: KING *and* QUEEN *enter.*

QUEEN: Tomorrow is Briar Rose's sixteenth birthday. We must be sure to warn her to stay in the castle until the sun sets.

KING: But we must not alarm her. She's grown into such a sweet young thing. All the fairies' wishes and gifts have come true. Let's hope Fairy Grundell's evil wish doesn't come to pass.

QUEEN: Hush . . . here comes our daughter now.

BRIAR ROSE (*Entering*): Good morning, Mother and Father.

QUEEN: Good morning, Briar Rose.

KING: You look so pretty today. And tomorrow you will be sixteen. Stay in the garden and close to the castle today, dear. (*To* QUEEN) Come, my dear, let's prepare for the celebration.

QUEEN: Come in soon, dear.

BRIAR ROSE: I will. (KING *and* QUEEN *exit.*) I wonder why they were so concerned?

HEDGEHOG (*Appearing*): Good morning.

BRIAR ROSE: Why, it's a dear little hedgehog. Aren't you cute!

HEDGEHOG: Listen carefully, Princess. I am your friend. Beware of evil fairies, at least until after tomorrow.

BRIAR ROSE: I don't understand.

HEDGEHOG: I don't mean to alarm you, but be careful. Goodbye for now — until we meet again.

BRIAR ROSE: Goodbye, friend. (*He exits.* BLACK CAT *enters from opposite side of stage.*) Oh, look at that beautiful kitty. Here, kitty!

BLACK CAT: Meow ... Good morning, Princess.

BRIAR ROSE: You can talk! What a strange garden this is!

CAT: Come and play with me. Meow-w-w.

BRIAR ROSE: What shall we do?

CAT: Let's explore the castle's towers.

BRIAR ROSE: What a delightful idea! Lead on, kitty. (*They exit. Curtain*)

*   *   *   *   *

SCENE 4

BEFORE RISE: NARRATOR *addresses audience.*

NARRATOR: And so the black cat led Briar Rose into the topmost tower of the castle. (*Exits. Curtain opens.*)

*   *   *   *   *

SETTING: *The interior of old tower.*

AT RISE: FAIRY GRUNDELL *stands by window. Spinning wheel and bed are at right.* CAT *enters.*

FAIRY GRUNDELL: Cat! Sixteen years have passed and the King and Queen still think their precious princess is safe from harm. (*Singing to tune of "Pop! Goes the Weasel"*)
    Sixteen years have hurried by
    It's time for her to perish.
    All she has to do then is die.
    Spin, spinning wheel.

(*Spinning wheel turns by itself.*)
>   Just to touch this poisoned pin,
>   That's all she has to do.
>   So hurry on, dear Briar Rose.
>   Spin, spinning wheel.

(*She cackles as spinning wheel turns.*)

CAT: Meow-w-w.

FAIRY GRUNDELL: Come over to me, cat. Little do they know I'm here and have the last remaining spinning wheel after all these years.

BRIAR ROSE (*Offstage*): Here, kitty. Where are you?

FAIRY GRUNDELL: Ah! I hear the Princess outside the door. Good work, cat! (*She sits on bed and spins.* BRIAR ROSE *enters.*)

BRIAR ROSE: Oh. There you are, kitty. Oh! (*Sees* FAIRY GRUNDELL) Excuse me. I didn't know anyone was up here.

FAIRY GRUNDELL (*Sweetly*): Come in, my dear.

BRIAR ROSE: I thought I knew everyone who worked here, but I don't think I've met you.

FAIRY GRUNDELL: I am just a flax maid for the Queen and this is where I work. Do not stop me because I must spin this whole basket of flax by the end of the day. (*She sighs and continues to spin.*)

BRIAR ROSE: Please, let me help you, you poor old soul. You must be very tired. Show me how and I'll spin for you. I've never seen a spinning wheel before.

FAIRY GRUNDELL: As you wish, my dear. It's very simple. All you have to do is turn the wheel and twist the flax on this point.

BRIAR ROSE (*Sitting at wheel*): Like this? (*She turns wheel.*)

FAIRY GRUNDELL: And one hand on the spindle.

BRIAR ROSE: Oh, I see. (*She pricks her finger.*) Oh! I stuck my finger! Oh, my goodness. I'm so sleepy. I ... (*She falls asleep on bed.*)

FAIRY GRUNDELL (*Laughing wildly*): Princess Briar Rose is dead! This will teach them not to overlook Fairy Grundell. (*She goes to window.*) Look, cat! They are preparing for her sixteenth birthday. Wait until they find her. (*She laughs.*)

CAT: Meow-w-w . . .

FAIRY GOLDEN (*Entering*): Evil Fairy Grundell. Be off with you!

FAIRY GRUNDELL: Fairy Golden! What are you doing here?

FAIRY GOLDEN: Briar Rose hasn't died, but only sleeps. I will surround the palace with a high briar hedge and after one hundred years the Princess will be awakened by the kiss of a handsome Prince. All the members of the court will also sleep and awaken at the same time.

FAIRY GRUNDELL: Just to make things interesting for this Prince, I will turn myself into a horrible dragon to keep him out. (*She laughs and exits with* CAT.)

FAIRY GOLDEN: Sleep, fair Princess, and await your true Prince. Goodbye! (*Curtain*)

*   *   *   *   *

SCENE 5

BEFORE RISE: NARRATOR *addresses audience.*

NARRATOR: Everyone in the palace fell fast asleep. Round the castle a hedge of briar grew. It grew so high that one could see only the topmost towers. Fairy Grundell turned herself into an ugly dragon and roamed about the hedge keeping young princes away. When one hundred years passed, a handsome Prince, who had heard the legend of the beautiful Sleeping Beauty, came to see if he could find her. (*Exits. Curtain opens.*)

*   *   *   *   *

SETTING: *Same as Scenes 1 and 3, except there is tall hedge of briar roses covering back of stage.*
AT RISE: DRAGON *enters.*

DRAGON: Beware, all strangers. Beware! One hundred years have passed. One hundred years! Sss-s-s-s. (*Exits*)
PRINCE (*Entering*): This must be the castle where a princess is supposed to sleep, though I can hardly see the roof or towers. This briar hedge grows so high. (*He touches the hedge.*) Those thorns are very sharp. I shall have to cut them away with my sword. (DRAGON *roars loudly offstage.*)
PRINCE: What was that?
DRAGON (*Offstage*): Go away, stranger, lest you lose your life.
PRINCE: Who threatens me?
DRAGON (*Offstage*): Go away and leave us in peace.
PRINCE: Whoever speaks, show yourself. I intend to wake Sleeping Beauty.
DRAGON (*Offstage*): So-o-o . . . another victim for the briar hedge — take care. (*The* DRAGON *enters and noisy battle takes place, with much clashing and moaning. The* PRINCE *kills* DRAGON.)
DRAGON (*Moaning*): Oh-h-h, fair Prince. You have won. The one hundred years have passed . . . and Fairy Grundell . . . is . . . no . . . more. (*Makes hissing sound, then expires.*)
PRINCE: The dragon is dead, but how will I ever get through this thick briar hedge?
HEDGEHOG (*Entering*): Good Prince, follow me. This briar patch has been my home and I know a way through to the castle.
PRINCE: Lead on, Sir Hedgehog. (*They exit. If desired,*

hedge may be lowered as curtains close. See Production Notes.)

* * * * *

SCENE 6

BEFORE RISE: NARRATOR *addresses audience.*

NARRATOR: The Prince entered the castle and saw the horses and hounds lying asleep in the courtyard. All the members of the court were asleep as well, in the same position they had taken when the spell was first placed upon them one hundred years before. The Prince roamed the castle halls until at last he reached the tower. He opened the door into the little room where Briar Rose slept.

* * *

SETTING: *Same as Scene 4.*

AT RISE: BRIAR ROSE *is still asleep on bed near window.* PRINCE *enters.*

PRINCE: This is the last room of the castle. Everyone and everything asleep. The Princess must be here somewhere. (*He sees her.*) Another sleeper yet. How beautiful . . . this must be Sleeping Beauty. (*He kisses her.*)

BRIAR ROSE (*Waking up*): I must have dozed off for a moment. (*Yawns*) Excuse me. Do you work here in the palace too?

PRINCE: One hundred years have passed since you and the others in the castle fell asleep. I have come to awaken you.

BRIAR ROSE: Thank you, dear Prince. (*Looking out window*) Look! Everyone else was asleep. But now they're awake as well. (KING *and* QUEEN *enter.*)

QUEEN: Dear Briar Rose, my child. Are you all right?

KING: The spell is broken. Thank you, good Prince.

QUEEN: What if Fairy Grundell returns?

PRINCE: She turned herself into a dragon and I killed her. She won't bother you anymore.

KING: Our Princess has been saved. (*To* PRINCE) Now for the marriage of you, good Prince, and you, dear daughter.

NARRATOR: So the handsome Prince saved the Princess from the evil spell. On the next day all was made ready for the grand marriage of Prince Charming and Briar Rose, our Sleeping Beauty. (*All puppets may appear, including* HEDGEHOG, *in tableau of wedding, as curtain closes.*)

THE END

Production Notes

SLEEPING BEAUTY

Number of Puppets: 11 hand or rod puppets or marionettes.

Characters: 1 male or female for Narrator.

Playing Time: 15 minutes.

Description of Puppets: Use your imagination for the puppets. Fairy tale books will give you costume ideas. Queen is beautiful and the King handsome. He might have a short beard so that he looks older than Prince. Briar Rose is pretty and wears an attractive gown. Good fairies wear gowns colored according to their names. Grundell is an old woman and wears a dark gown. Dragon should be fierce and menacing.

Properties: None required.

Setting: Scenes 1 and 3: The castle garden. Background shows flowers, statues, part of castle. Scene 2: The throne room, with baby crib, thrones. Scenes 4 and 6: The tower, a dark room with a single window, a simple bed, and spinning wheel, baskets of flax (white yarn). Scene 5: The castle garden, with high hedge across back of stage, hiding corner of castle.

Lighting: No special effects.

Sound: Music from Tchaikovsky's "Sleeping Beauty" may be used.

Special Effects: The hedge wall may be drawn on soft material and lowered at the end of Scene 5 when Dragon dies. Put the wall on a long rod across top of stage and lower it on two strings. The spinning wheel should turn by itself. You can wind a long cord around the side of the wheel and pull from below or above, or you can make a treadmill cord on a handle from above or below.

THE THREE LITTLE PIGS

Characters

MOTHER PIG
THREE LITTLE PIGS
BIG BAD WOLF

SCENE 1

SETTING: *Outside Mother Pig's house.*
AT RISE: MOTHER PIG *and* THREE LITTLE PIGS *enter.*
MOTHER PIG *is sniffing and crying.*

MOTHER PIG: I'm afraid I have some bad news for you, my dear little piggies. I have become so poor that I can no longer take care of you. You must leave to make your own way in this big, cruel world.

1ST PIG: Oh — what shall we do?

2ND PIG: That sounds awful!

3RD PIG: I'm sorry, Mother dear, but we understand. Is there some way that we can help you?

2ND PIG: Just so it's not too much work!

MOTHER PIG: Why, yes. You must each build yourself your own separate home, where you will be safe and secure from that nasty, hungry wolf who lives in the forest.

3RD PIG: Of course, Mother. That is not too much to ask.

1ST PIG: It will be nice to have my own house — where I can do just as I please.

2ND PIG: Yes. And we're not afraid of that silly old wolf. He won't catch us.

75

MOTHER PIG: Now, now, children. You must beware of that big bad wolf. He is clever — and always hungry! You must promise to build yourselves good strong houses, so he won't be able to get inside and catch you for his dinner.

1ST PIG: Have no fear. We're big boys now. You won't have to worry about me! Goodbye. I'll follow that road to the left. (*He exits.*)

2ND PIG: Goodbye. I'll take that trail to the right. I'm positive that's the best. (*He exits.*)

MOTHER PIG (*To* 3RD PIG): And you, my son, what do you plan to do?

3RD PIG: Well, Mother, I have always enjoyed bakin' and cookin' — so I think I'll open a little inn near Lake Huffenpuff.

MOTHER PIG: That's nice. Be a good pig — and come see your mama once in a while. (*Cries*) Boo-hoo ...

3RD PIG: Don't cry, Mother. I won't forget you. I will follow that path there — the straight and narrow one. Goodbye. (*Curtain*)

*   *   *   *   *

SCENE 2

SETTING: *A field with haystacks.*
AT RISE: 1ST PIG *enters.*

1ST PIG: This looks like a good place to settle down. There's plenty of food to eat in that farmer's field and I won't have to build a house. I'll just hollow out a haystack and then live inside. That won't take any work at all. (*He hollows out haystack.*) There! Instant housing. And I'll just put a board across the door ... (*He goes inside and hangs board across opening. Speaking from behind stack*) Oh! Such a genius! Now I'll just take a nap. (WOLF *enters, carrying suitcase labeled* FULLER BRUSH.)

WOLF: Are my eyes deceiving me, or did I see a fat little piggie crawl into that haystack? (*Calling*) Yoo-hoo! Any fat little piggies at home?

1ST PIG: Oh-oh. Who is it, please?

WOLF: It's just me, your friendly Fuller Brush man. Come out so I can show you my wares.

1ST PIG: No, thanks. I have enough brushes. Good day.

WOLF: I said, come out of there!

1ST PIG: I can't. I'm in the middle of something.

WOLF: If you can't come out, let me come in.

1ST PIG: Oh, no, no. Not by the hair of my chinny-chin-chin.

WOLF: Then I'll huff and I'll puff, and I'll blow your house in. (WOLF *blows hard and loud and haystack disappears, revealing* 1ST PIG.) Ah-ha! Now I gotcha — a — a — a choo! Oh, *no!* I forgot about my hay fever. (*Sneezes loudly*) A — a — a . . .

1ST PIG: Oh-oh — I'd better get, while the getting's good. (*He runs off.*)

WOLF: Choo-o-o! Come back here. (*He runs after* 1ST PIG. *Curtain.*)

* * * * *

SCENE 3

SETTING: *A forest.*

AT RISE: 2ND PIG *enters.*

2ND PIG: I must have walked miles. And still I haven't found a deserted house. I guess I'll have to build my own after all. Let me see. (*Picks branches from ground.*) Here are some branches. I'll just build a house out of them. (*He builds house of branches.*) There! And I'll use this old plank for a door. (*He hangs plank over door opening.*)

1ST PIG (*Appearing*): Oh, brother, you must save me! The Wolf is after me. He is going to eat me.

2ND PIG: I knew you wouldn't be able to take care of yourself. You can stay here tonight, but after that you'll have to pay rent.

1ST PIG: Yes, yes. Quick, inside. Here comes the Wolf. (*Both enter house and close door with plank, just as* WOLF *enters.*)

WOLF: I saw you go in there! Both of you. Now I'll have two little pigs instead of just one for dinner. (*Calls*) Little pigs, little pigs, let me come in!

PIGS (*From inside house*): No, no, no. Not by the hair of our chinny-chin-chins.

WOLF: Eh? I didn't hear you. What did you say?

PIGS (*From inside house*): No, no, no. Not by the hair of our chinny-chin-chins!

WOLF: In that case, I'll huff and I'll puff and I'll blow your house in. (WOLF *blows three times; house falls down and door plank hits* WOLF *on nose.* PIGS *are revealed.*) Ow-w — oh, my nose. That door hit my poor sensitive nose.

2ND PIG: Quick, let's get away from here. (*They run away.*)

WOLF: Come back! Oh-h! My nose! (*He chases after them. Curtain.*)

*   *   *   *   *

SCENE 4

SETTING: *Cutaway view of inside of 3rd Pig's brick house, showing door, window, and fireplace, and area outside near door.*

AT RISE: 3RD PIG *is putting finishing touches on outside of house.*

3RD PIG: There! All finished! I was very lucky to find that pile of old bricks to use for my house. It was hard work building this place, but I have a feeling it will be worth it. (*Looking off*) Oh-oh! Here comes trouble. (1ST *and* 2ND PIGS *enter.*)

1ST PIG: Quick! Hide us!

2ND PIG: He'll eat us all. He's so big and ferocious!

3RD PIG: Who is after you?

1ST PIG: The Wolf! The big bad Wolf!

3RD PIG: We have nothing to fear. I followed Mother's advice and built a strong brick house for myself.

2ND PIG: But he'll blow it in, just like he did ours.

3RD PIG: That I'll have to see with my own eyes, brothers. Come on. I will give you something to eat. (PIGS *enter house and close door.*)

WOLF (*Appearing outside house*): Hm-m-m. This time I'll use the old noggin. I'll trick them into letting me in. (*He knocks on door.*)

3RD PIG: Who's there?

WOLF (*In falsetto*): It's me, Granny Goosekins. I've got nice fresh eggs for sale. Open the door. (*Peeks in window*)

3RD PIG: No, thanks. We don't need any.

WOLF (*Still in falsetto*): Oh, but these are special extra-large eggs. And — er — magic, too!

3RD PIG: No, thanks. And besides, you don't fool me one bit — you big, bad Wolf . . .

WOLF (*In normal voice*): Curses. I thought sure I'd get an Oscar for that performance. (*To* PIGS) O.K., open the door. little piggie-pig-pigs, or I'll blow your house in.

PIGS (*Together*): No, no, no! Not by the hair of our chinny-chin-chins.

WOLF: If that's the way you want it. (*Huffs and puffs*) Hm-m-m! I don't seem to be getting anywhere. (*Huffs and puffs*) They don't build houses like they used to! (*Huffs and puffs*) Aw, come on, you guys. Open the door and let me in.

PIGS (*Together*): No, no, no! Not by the hair of our chinny-chin-chins.

WOLF: Sorry I asked. Now what'll I do? (*Thinks*) Ah-*ha!* (*Calling*) Little piggies, I'm sorry I've been so bad. Just to make it up to you, let me take you to the county fair tomorrow. They're selling nice fresh turnips there, and we can stop at Farmer Brown's orchard on the way to pick some big red apples.

1ST PIG: Sounds yummy.

2ND PIG: I can't wait.

3RD PIG: What time shall we meet you there?

WOLF: Ten o'clock tomorrow morning.

3RD PIG: We'll be there! (*Aside*) Only *much* earlier!

WOLF: Goody! Until tomorrow, goodbye. (*As he exits*) Oh, boy — fresh bacon, pigs' knuckles and pork chops. Yum! (*He exits. Curtain.*)

*   *   *   *   *

SCENE 5

SETTING: *Farmer Brown's orchard. Apple trees are placed about, including one cut-out for climbing. Back drop shows county fair.*

AT RISE: PIGS *enter.* 3RD PIG *has basket of turnips on his arm.*

3RD PIG: We had a very nice time at the fair, and I have a basketful of fresh turnips for supper. Now we had better return home. It's almost ten o'clock and the Wolf will be here soon.

1ST PIG: Oh, we have ten minutes yet. And besides, he promised to be nice. I'm having too much fun to go. I'm going back and ride the merry-go-round. (*He exits.*)

3RD PIG (*To* 2ND PIG): How about you? Ready to go?

2ND PIG: No. I think I'll pick some of those nice red apples over there. I'm hungry.

3RD PIG: Very well, but remember — whatever the Wolf said, he is hungry, too! (*Exits*)

2ND PIG: Goodbye, and good riddance. Always telling us what to do. Who does he think he is? I can take care of myself. I'll just climb this tree and eat some of those lovely apples. (*Climbs tree*)

WOLF (*Entering*): Ten o'clock on the dot. But I don't see those pigs. Where could they be?

1ST PIG (*Entering with big kettle*): Yoo-hoo! Mister Wolf! Here I am. Look what I won at the fair — a big cooking kettle.

WOLF: How nice. But where are your brothers?

1ST PIG: They didn't believe that you changed your ways and they left for home.

WOLF: Too bad. But there's still you, isn't there?

1ST PIG: Yes. Here I am!

WOLF: So I see. Well! Ah . . . and what's inside your kettle?

1ST PIG: Why, nothing, I guess.

WOLF: You mean you're not sure? Then you'd better check. It might be filled with money — or food — or . . .

1ST PIG: Good idea. (*He bends over pot and* WOLF *pushes him in.*) Let me out! Let me out!

2ND PIG (*From tree*): Oh, help! Help! The big bad Wolf has my brother.

WOLF: What's this? A flying pig? Up there in the apple tree! (WOLF *shakes tree and* 2ND PIG *falls out.*)

2ND PIG: Help! Help! Oh, I've eaten too much. I can't run!

WOLF: Got you, too! (*Picks up* 2ND PIG *and puts him into pot*) Now just one more to go and my pantry will be full! (*He runs out with pot. Curtain*)

*   *   *   *   *

SCENE 6

SETTING: *The same as Scene 4. There is a pitcher near fire-place.*

AT RISE: 3RD PIG *is inside his house.* WOLF *enters with pot.*

WOLF (*Calling*): Little pig! Little pig! Open the door and let me in.

3RD PIG (*Aside*): Oh, not again. (*Calling*) No, no, no — not by the hair of my chinny-chin-chin.

WOLF: Oh, please let me in. I can't blow down your house!

1ST *and* 2ND PIGS (*In pot*): Help! Help! Let us out!

3RD PIG: Who was that? Who is out there with you?

WOLF: Oh, er — just an old chicken I have in my pot.

3RD PIG: Chicken? Oh, I just love chicken. And I need a pot for cooking. I'll make a bargain with you. You shove the pot through my window and I'll tell you a secret way to get into my house.

WOLF: You will? O.K. It's a deal. Here. (WOLF *shoves pot through window*) Now — how do I get in?

3RD PIG: Why — down the chimney, of course.

WOLF: Oh, goodie. But how do I get on the roof?

3RD PIG: There's a ladder in the barn about a mile down the road.

WOLF: Oh, boy. Now don't go away. I'll be right back. (*He exits.* 3RD PIG *pulls* 1ST *and* 2ND PIGS *from pot*)

1ST PIG: Saved at last!

2ND PIG: Yes, but the Wolf is coming down the chimney. What shall we do?

3RD PIG: Quick! Put some boiling water into the pot and put it in the fireplace.

1ST PIG: Like this? (*Pretends to pour water from pitcher into pot.*)

3RD PIG: Yes — that will do it. It's brim full. Quick! Put the pot in the fireplace. (*They put pot into fireplace.*)

WOLF (*From offstage*): Yoo-hoo! (*Enters, carrying ladder*) Little piggies! Here I come.... (*Props ladder against house, climbs up to chimney on roof*)

1ST PIG: Here he comes now! (WOLF *jumps into chimney, falls down into pot of boiling water.*)

WOLF: Help! (*Disappears into pot*)

3RD PIG: The Wolf is gone.

1ST PIG: Oh, brother, you saved us. May we stay here and live with you?

3RD PIG: Why, yes, but you have to earn your keep.

1ST PIG: Well — O.K.

2ND PIG: I guess it's the least we can do.

3RD PIG: Yes . . . and it probably will be. (1ST *and* 2ND PIGS *exit. To audience*) So we three little pigs lived happily ever after — in our house that is completely wolf-proof — and that, children, is quite a pig's feat! (*Curtain*)

THE END

Production Notes

The Three Little Pigs

Number of Puppets: 5 hand puppets.

Playing Time: 15 minutes.

Description of Puppets: The Pigs wear shabby, patched clothes, and they should wear different hats to make them easily identifiable. Wolf should have baggy pants held up by one suspender.

Properties: Basket of turnips, large pot, branches, suitcase, pitcher, ladder.

Setting: Scene 1: A backdrop showing Mother's house. Scene 2: A field with haystack backdrop. Pig's haystack is a simple cardboard cut-out with an opening for Pig (or he may simply disappear behind it). Scene 3: A forest backdrop. House is made of cardboard, and may be pushed up slowly from below as Pig "builds" it with branches. Both houses have nails on which cardboard doors may be hung. Scenes 4 and 6: Interior of brick house, with working door, fireplace and cut-out window. Fireplace has opening so wolf puppet may be dropped from above into pot. Scene 5: An orchard, with county fair backdrop. An apple tree cut from cardboard is hung from side of stage. When puppet "climbs" tree, it actually leaves stage. When Pigs are pushed into pot, they drop behind pot out of sight.

Lighting: No special effects.

THE EMPEROR'S NIGHTINGALE

Adapted from a story by Hans Christian Andersen

Characters

FISHERMAN
FIRST MINISTER
DOCTOR
LITTLE COOK
NIGHTINGALE
EMPEROR
JAPANESE COURIER
DEATH

SCENE 1

SETTING: *A small forest beside a river in China.*
AT RISE: FISHERMAN *appears in his boat and floats across stage.*

FISHERMAN (*Reciting*):
>Let me tell of the nightingale
>Who sang for the Emperor of China.
>Nowhere did any bird sing more beautifully or
>   finer.
>Watch closely now and let's unfold (*Throws out net*)
>A wonderful tale, once again told,
>For grown-up and for minor.

(*Pulls in net and he and boat float off.* DOCTOR *and* FIRST MINISTER *come in.*)

DOCTOR: This is where we are to meet the little cook, here in the woods by the stream.

MINISTER: I know all about the world. I don't know why we have to ask a lowly cook.

DOCTOR: The Emperor wishes to hear the nightingale sing. Only this cook knows of the bird.

MINISTER: Here she comes now. (LITTLE COOK *enters and bows.*)

COOK: Good afternoon, Your Excellencies. You wish to hear the nightingale? Its song will bring tears to your eyes, it's so beautiful.

DOCTOR: Your Emperor wishes to hear its beautiful singing. Find the bird for us and you will have a permanent place in the Emperor's kitchen and permission to see the Emperor dine.

MINISTER: The bird is commanded to appear at court tonight. Quickly, point it out to us.

COOK: The nightingale lives right here in these woods. Now, listen carefully. (*Sound of cow mooing is heard.*)

MINISTER: That must be the nightingale. What remarkable power for such a small creature.

COOK: Oh, no. That's a cow mooing. (*Sound of frogs croaking is heard.*)

DOCTOR: How beautiful! It sounds just like the tinkling of temple bells.

COOK: No. Those are just frogs croaking. We shall soon hear the little bird. (*Melodious bird song is heard.*) Listen, listen! There it is. (NIGHTINGALE *flies in.*) See? There it is!

MINISTER: Is it possible? I should never have thought it would look like that. How common it looks. Seeing such important people as us must have frightened away all its colors.

COOK: Little nightingale, our gracious Emperor wishes you to sing for him tonight.

NIGHTINGALE: With the greatest of pleasure, sweet little cook.

MINISTER: Quickly, then. It's time we were at court. We mustn't keep His Majesty waiting.

DOCTOR: All at court are anxious to hear you sing, little nightingale.

NIGHTINGALE: My voice sounds best here among the trees, but I am willing to go with you if the Emperor commands it.

COOK: Fly ahead, sweet little bird. We will follow. (NIGHT-INGALE *flies off, and others follow. Curtain*)

*   *   *   *   *

SCENE 2

SETTING: *The palace courtyard, decorated with chimes, bells and lighted lanterns. Throne and stand are at center.*

AT RISE: *If desired, there may be a procession across stage, ending with* MINISTER *and* DOCTOR *and finally,* EMPEROR, *who sits on throne.*

MINISTER: O Great Emperor, ruler of the sun, king of the moon, after much research and hardship I have accomplished what you commanded, and wish to tell you that ...

EMPEROR: Get on with it. Have you found the nightingale?

MINISTER: Your Majesty, I have. I found him in ...

DOCTOR (*Interrupting*): The little cook from the royal kitchens led us to the bird that sings so beautifully. She has the nightingale.

MINISTER: Humph! Really!

EMPEROR: Allow the little maid to enter. I wish to see her and this nightingale. (DOCTOR *signals, and* COOK *enters with* NIGHTINGALE *on her hand. She bows deeply.*) Little cook, have the nightingale sing for me.

COOK: My Emperor, the nightingale is anxious to sing for you. (*She sets* NIGHTINGALE *on stand and exits.*)

NIGHTINGALE: I sing my song to please you, great ruler, and to make all the people on this earth happy.

MINISTER: Much too good for them.

DOCTOR: Quiet, First Minister. Sh-h-h.

NIGHTINGALE: My song is of the night and day ... of the spring and of the fall. Listen closely to my song. Think lovely thoughts. (*Bird song is heard.*)

EMPEROR (*Crying gently*): How beautiful. Why haven't I heard this nightingale before?

MINISTER: We have many birds in our forest.

DOCTOR: It has a fine warble, my Emperor.

EMPEROR (*Comes from throne, to* NIGHTINGALE): You sing so beautifully, my lovely little bird. (*Sniffs*) Thank you. Thank you! I award you the Medal of the Golden Slipper to wear round your neck.

NIGHTINGALE: I have been rewarded already. I see tears in the eyes of my Emperor. (*Sings again*)

EMPEROR: So beautiful! So beautiful! He will have a golden cage as well as twelve servants to wait on him beak and claw, and to walk him on a twenty-foot silken ribbon.

DOCTOR: How very delightful.

MINISTER: I can sing too ... listen! (*He gargles. All laugh.*) Humph! (*He exits.* JAPANESE COURIER *enters carrying mechanical bird on a music box.*)

COURIER: O great Chinese Emperor, I come from the great Japanese Emperor, who wishes to present this magnificent mechanical bird. It is a present for his great friend. (*He sets it down.*)

EMPEROR: Thank you, Courier. Send my best regards to your Emperor. A valuable present will return with you for him. Now play the instrument. Turn the key and let us hear the jeweled bird sing. (COURIER *turns key and bird song is heard.*)

ALL (*Ad lib*): How wonderful! Beautiful! Magnificent! (*Etc.* NIGHTINGALE *flies away but no one notices.*)

EMPEROR: Now let us hear the nightingale and compare.

DOCTOR: The nightingale has flown away.

MINISTER: Just as well. That ungrateful bird. As First Minister I banish the nightingale from the castle gardens. (*To* EMPEROR) The mechanical bird is the best bird of all.

EMPEROR: Then let us hear the mechanical bird again. (*Bird is wound up and it sings.*) Beautiful! Beautiful to hear and to look upon. Place it next to my bed, and it will be played every night at bedtime. (*Procession enters and mechanical bird is carried off. All exit, then* COOK *enters.*)

COOK (*Calling*): Nightingale! My sweet nightingale! Where are you? Come back! (*Curtain*)

* * * * *

SCENE 3

BEFORE RISE: FISHERMAN *enters in front of curtain.*

FISHERMAN (*Reciting*):
>The Emperor now as time has passed
>Lies sick abed, and breathes his last.
>Nightingale, fly to his side and bring
>The song that only you can sing. (*Exits. Curtains open.*)

* * *

SETTING: *The Emperor's bedroom. Mechanical bird is beside bed.*

AT RISE: EMPEROR *lies on bed.* DEATH, *wearing crown and holding scepter, sits at back of bed.* DOCTOR *and* COOK *are talking.*

COOK: Doctor, is there no cure for our great Emperor?

DOCTOR: Do you not see? Death sits beside him. I am afraid his time has come to leave us forever.

EMPEROR (*Weakly*): Doctor, wind the mechanical bird once more. Its song eases my pain.

DOCTOR: Yes, my Emperor. (*He winds bird, and birdsong is heard, then bird breaks apart with jangling sound.*) Oh, dear! I'm afraid the jeweled bird will never sing again. It is worn out. (DOCTOR *carries out bird.*)

EMPEROR: Worn out, just like me. Little cook, if I could only hear my nightingale once more. Find him for me.

COOK: I will try. (*She exits.*)

EMPEROR: O Spirit of Death, do not sit so heavy upon my chest. I am weary.

DEATH: It is almost time for you to come with me. (*Bird song is heard.*)

EMPEROR (*Sitting up a little*): Listen!

DEATH: How beautiful! (NIGHTINGALE *flies in.*)

EMPEROR: My nightingale returns.

DEATH: Sing again, sweet bird.

NIGHTINGALE: Give the Emperor back his crown, and I will sing.

DEATH: Yes, yes. (*Gives crown to* EMPEROR) Now sing, nightingale. (*Bird song is heard.*) I've never heard anything so beautiful before. Not here in this world or any other.

NIGHTINGALE: Give back the scepter.

DEATH: Yes, yes, only sing again. (*Returns scepter and bird song is heard*) Beautiful! Sing again!

NIGHTINGALE: Only if you give our Emperor back to us.

DEATH: Yes, yes. Only sing again. (*Bird song is heard.*) Now I will go. One of your songs is worth more than anything. Rise, Great Emperor. I shall come back another time, many years from now. Goodbye, little nightingale. (*Exits*)

EMPEROR: Thank you, heavenly little bird. I banished you from my sight, and yet now you have charmed even Death away from me. How can I ever repay you?

NIGHTINGALE: You have rewarded me. I brought tears to your eyes the very first time I sang for you, and I shall never forget it. Those tears are the jewels that gladden the heart of a singer. (*Bird song is heard.*)

EMPEROR: Now you must stay with me always. You shall sing only when you wish.

NIGHTINGALE: I cannot build my nest and live in this palace, but let me come to you whenever I like. Then I will sit on the branch outside your window in the evening and sing to you. I will sing to cheer you and to make you thoughtful, too. I will sing about the good and about the evil which are kept hidden from you. Only you must tell no one a little bird told you so. (NIGHTINGALE *exits.* EMPEROR *goes behind bed and is hidden from view.* DOCTOR *and* COOK *enter.*)

COOK (*Crying*): Our poor, poor Emperor. What is to become of us?

DOCTOR: It must be his time, little cook. Death is gone and so is our Emperor. Our poor, poor Emperor. (*He cries.*)

EMPEROR (*Coming out wearing crown and carrying scepter*): Look! I'm well again. Good morning, everyone!

DOCTOR *and* COOK: Long live the Emperor! (*Curtain*)

THE END

Production Notes

THE EMPEROR'S NIGHTINGALE

Number of Puppets: 8 hand or rod puppets or marionettes.
Playing Time: 15 minutes.
Description of Puppets: Books of Chinese costumes will suggest costuming for Emperor and his court. They should have long brocade robes in bright colors and elaborate headdresses. Fisherman and Cook wear simple short coolie coats and trousers. Fisherman might wear a large flat straw hat. Death might be tall and thin, wearing black robe. Nightingale can be a small toy bird on a wire, worked either from above or below.
Properties: Net, jeweled mechanical bird on a fancy music box with large key, crown and scepter, small boat, either a flat cut-out or a three-dimensional one.
Setting: Scene 1: A forest of bamboo and fir trees beside a river. Scene 2: The palace courtyard, with a throne and stand for nightingale, and decorated with chimes, bells and lanterns. If desired, just a fancy curtain may be used. Scene 3: Emperor's bedroom with large bed surrounded by curtains.
Lighting: No special effects, although Scenes 1 and 3 may be dim and Scene 2 bright and colorful.
Sound: Cow mooing, frogs croaking, melodious bird song (either a sound effects record of bird calls or done live by someone who can whistle like a bird). The breaking of mechanical bird can be done by jumbling kitchen utensils together. If desired, recorded Chinese music may be used, or Stravinsky's "The Emperor and the Nightingale."

AESOP'S FABLES

Characters

NARRATOR
AESOP
THREE CHILDREN
HARE
TORTOISE
ANT
GRASSHOPPER
LION
MOUSE

SCENE 1

SETTING: *A path leading to a Greek village, which is visible in background.*

AT RISE: NARRATOR *addresses audience.*

NARRATOR: Once, many, many years ago, there was a wonderful old man by the name of Aesop, who lived in Greece. He was famous for telling delightful stories about animals, and all the children knew him. One day, as he was walking down the road.... (AESOP *enters, on path.* HARE *hops in, and* AESOP *stops to pet it.*)

AESOP: Well.... What have we here? Hello, Mr. Hare. Have you had any close races lately? (HARE *runs off, as* THREE CHILDREN *enter.*)

1ST CHILD: Oh, look! There's Aesop. Come on, let's ask him to tell us a story.

2ND CHILD: Oh, yes. I love his stories. They're always so exciting.

3RD CHILD: I'd rather go swimming.

1ST CHILD: Oh, come on. We can swim later.

2ND CHILD: Yoo-hoo, Mr. Aesop. Would you tell us another one of your exciting tales today?

AESOP: Hello, there. I don't seem to have anything else on my list of things to do today.... So sit here beside me and tell me which story you'd like to hear.

1ST CHILD: How about the Tortoise and the Hare?

2ND CHILD: I like the one about the Lion and the Mouse.

3RD CHILD: They're dumb. I like the one about the Grass-hopper and the Ant.

AESOP: My, my. Suppose I tell you all three?

2ND CHILD: All three?

1ST CHILD: Wow!

3RD CHILD: Just so you tell the one about the grasshopper.

AESOP: Oh, I will, lad, I will. Now let me see.... Where shall I start? Oh, yes. Once upon a time there was a very boastful rabbit who lived in the forest. He was a very fast rabbit, and he knew it. And he let everyone else know it, too. (AESOP *and* CHILDREN *exit.* HARE *comes hopping in.*)

HARE (*Singing or reciting*):
Hop, hop, hop, catch me if you can.
Hop, hop, hop, yes, it is my plan.
Faster than a deer or cheetah,
Faster than a small mosquito —
Hop, hop, hop — here I go again.

Hop, hop, hop, catch me if you will.
Hop, hop, hop, up and down the hill.
I am faster than a sparrow,

Faster than a speeding arrow —
Hop, hop, hop, catch me if you will.

(TORTOISE *appears.*) Well, look who's here. Hello, there, Brother Tortoise. Where are you going?

TORTOISE (*Speaking slowly*): Oh, hello, Brother Hare. I am going to the garage to get a shine.

HARE: To the garage to get a shine?

TORTOISE: Yes, I heard that they have a new kind of turtle wax.

HARE: Turtle wax? Shine? Oh, ho, ho! That's a good one. Maybe you can have them wax the bottoms of your feet. That might make you move a little faster.

TORTOISE: I'm doing just fine, thank you.

HARE: Fine? Why, at the rate you're going, it'll take you two days just to get to the village, and another day to reach the garage.

TORTOISE: At least I always get where I am going.

HARE: That might have been all right twenty years ago, but today you have to have speed. (*Sings to the tune of "You've Gotta Have Heart"*)

> You have to have spee-e-e-e-eeed,
> Lots and lots and lots of speed,
> Yes, today you simply have to be fast, or
> You're bound to be passed and left behind.
> So you have to have speed,
> To do just my kind of deed,
> Or you'll be left far behind.

TORTOISE: Hogwash! With all your bragging and boasting, you're the one that's likely to be left behind. Slow and steady always wins out.

HARE: Aha! What's this I hear? Was that a challenge to a race?

TORTOISE: Why, I only mentioned . . . .

HARE: I accept. We'll start here, and the garage will be the finish line. You just keep moving along. I'll run ahead and tell everyone about the race. . .get the judges,. . .the spectators. . .and then I'll come back. You should be over by that tree by then. (*Laughs*) Goodbye. (*Runs off*)

TORTOISE (*Shouting*): Hey, wait a minute! (*Lowering voice*) I don't even feel like racing. Oh, well, I suppose I could go a little faster. (ANT *appears, dragging a large bag, and bumps into* TORTOISE.)

ANT: Hey, watch where you're going.

TORTOISE: Oh, I'm sorry, Ant. My mind wasn't on where I was going.

ANT: You made me spill some of my crumbs. I have to get these into storage before winter gets here.

TORTOISE: Winter? Winter is still weeks away.

ANT: One can never be too well prepared for the future.

TORTOISE: True — one may be "hare" today, and gone tomorrow. (*Starts to go off*)

ANT: What's your big hurry? Stop a minute and talk while I pick up my crumbs.

TORTOISE: Oh, I can't. I'm in a race.

ANT: A race? You? You must be kidding.

TORTOISE: Oh, no. I wouldn't kid you. I'm racing brother Hare to the village garage.

ANT: Good luck — you'll need it. I hope you do beat that bragger!

TORTOISE: Thank you. Goodbye. (*Starts off, slowly, singing to tune of "Old MacDonald Had a Farm," verse only*)

> I may be slow, but this I know,
> I get where I am going.
> In spite of wind, in spite of rain,
> Or even though it's snowing.

I just keep moving right along,

For this fact I am knowing,

I may be slow, but this I know,

I get where I am going. (*Exits*)

ANT: Well, well.... He may make it, at that!

GRASSHOPPER (*Entering*): Howdy, Ant. What's in that bag? Food, I hope!

ANT: Yes, Grasshopper, it's food. But not food to eat now. I'm taking it to my warehouse to store until winter.

GRASSHOPPER: That's silly. All that food just sitting there. Let's eat!

ANT: No, the food stays in the bag. There's plenty of food now, all around you. Help me carry this bag to my warehouse, and I'll help you find some food in the fields.

GRASSHOPPER: No, thanks. That bag looks heavy. I think I'll just go off into the woods and play my violin. And maybe sing, too. (*Sings or recites*)

I like to dance and sing and play.

My singing's good, or so they say.

I dance and sing and play all day

Because I like to be that way. (*Exits*)

ANT: Some help he is. One of these days, he'll be sorry. Oh, well, I had better get moving. It seems to be getting colder. Maybe winter isn't that far away. (*Pulling bag*) Ugh! This sure is heavy. (*Exits with bag.* MOUSE *enters.*)

MOUSE: Do I smell food? I do! Nice fresh crumbs all over the ground. (*Eats*) And good, too!

LION (*Offstage*): Roar!

MOUSE (*Looking up*): What was that?

LION (*Offstage*): *Roar!*

MOUSE: It sounded like a roar.

LION (*Offstage*): ROAR!

MOUSE: It was a roar, and it came from those bushes over there. (*He pulls aside bushes.* LION *is entangled in net.*)

Well, who have we here? Is that a hairnet you're wearing, brother Lion?

LION: No, it's not a hairnet, it's a hunter's net, and I'm caught in it. Can you help me?

MOUSE: Under ordinary circumstances, I don't think I would. You are a member of the *cat* family, you know. But you did spare my life the other day when you caught me, so I see no reason why you would eat me now. Besides, I owe you a favor.

LION: The net! Chew the net!

MOUSE: I know.... I'll chew the net. (*Starts to gnaw*)

LION: I think you're getting it.

MOUSE: There — it's loose.

LION (*Coming out of net*): Free! Free! I'm free! (*Recites*)
    Free, free, I'm finally free.
    Free from the net that held me so tight.
    Free from the fleas and mosquitoes that bite,
    Free, free, I'm finally free.
    Isn't it wonderful — just you and me
    And we're free, free, free!

MOUSE: You're welcome, I'm sure.

LION: Oh, thank you, little fellow. And remember, you're my pal now. If anybody gives you any trouble, just whistle. Goodbye. (*Exits*)

MOUSE: Sure, sure. Any time. Goodbye. (*Looking about*) Now, I wonder if there are more crumbs down the road? (*Exits. Curtain*)

*   *   *   *   *

SCENE 2

SETTING: *Outside Ant's warehouse.*

AT RISE: ANT *enters, dragging bag.* TORTOISE *follows him in slowly.*

TORTOISE (*Singing*):
> I may be slow, but this I know,
> I get where I am going.

(*Puffing*) I'd better slow down a bit. I'm getting tired.

ANT: Yoo-hoo! Tortoise, could you help me with my bag? It's getting so heavy.

TORTOISE: I shouldn't stop right now.

ANT: Why on earth not?

TORTOISE: Because I'm in a race — remember?

ANT: Oh, yes. The race. (*Laughs*)

TORTOISE: It's not funny. That bragging bunny tricked me into racing with him, and I'd like to win, just to teach him a lesson.

ANT: I wish I could help, but I don't see how. But, please, can you help *me* put this bag of crumbs into my storehouse? It won't take long.

TORTOISE: Very well. You pull and I'll push. (*They push bag into doorway of warehouse.*) Ugh! Ooof!

ANT: Oh-h-h! There! It's halfway in, but I think it's stuck.

TORTOISE (*Pushing*): It won't budge any further.

ANT: Oh, dear. What shall I do? I can't just leave it out like that. (MOUSE *enters.*)

MOUSE: Hello, there. Having trouble?

ANT: Yes. I can't seem to get my bag of crumbs through the doorway.

MOUSE: Bag of crumbs, did you say? Yum, yum. Well, maybe I can help. If I gnaw a little hole in the side of the bag, and let some of the crumbs spill out, maybe the bag will fit.

ANT: But those are my crumbs for winter.

MOUSE: It's the only way I can see. Just let me have the few crumbs that spill out, and I'll do the job.

ANT: O.K., it's a deal.

MOUSE: I'll gnaw here...

ANT: And I'll crawl over the top and pull from the inside...

TORTOISE: I'd better get back to my race. Good luck, Ant.

ANT: Thank you, good luck to you, too.

TORTOISE (*Singing to tune of "Old MacDonald Had a Farm"*):
> I may be slow, but this I know,
> I know where I am going... (*Exits*)

ANT (*Crawling inside warehouse*): All right, you gnaw, and I'll pull.

MOUSE (*Gnawing*): O.K., I've gnawed a nice little hole, and some crumbs have spilled out. You pull.

ANT (*From inside warehouse*): I'm pulling. (GRASSHOPPER *and* HARE *enter.*)

HARE: Well, what have we here?

GRASSHOPPER: It smells like food to me.

HARE: I could do with a snack before I continue my race.

GRASSHOPPER: Care to join me?

HARE: Don't mind if I do. (*Pushing* MOUSE *aside*) One side, there, Mouse. Let us hungry guys eat.

MOUSE: This food doesn't belong to you. Go away and earn your own crumbs.

HARE: I said, *step aside,* Mouse, or I'll thump you into the ground.

GRASSHOPPER: You heard him, Mouse.

MOUSE: I won't.

HARE: Very well, then. I'll just... (MOUSE *whistles, and* LION *appears.*)

LION: Did you whistle for me, brother Mouse?

MOUSE: Yes, these two loafers want to take the Ant's hard-earned food away from her.

LION: Oh, they do, do they? (*Advances toward* HARE *and* GRASSHOPPER) We'll see about that.

HARE: Um, er, we were just going.

GRASSHOPPER: Yes, we're not so hungry after all.

HARE *and* GRASSHOPPER: Goodbye! (*They race off.*)

LION (*Calling after them*): And don't come back, or you may end up being *my* food! (*Laughs*)

MOUSE: Thank you, brother Lion. What would we do without friends? Now, let's just push this bag into the warehouse. (*They push and bag goes in.*)

ANT (*From warehouse*): It worked. The bag's in. (ANT *comes out.*) Thank you both for your help. Now if we could only help the Tortoise win his race!

LION: Race? What race?

ANT: That bragging Hare challenged the Tortoise to a race that ends at the garage.

LION: Hmm. Well, I'll run ahead and see if I can be of any help.

MOUSE: Maybe you can be the finish "lion." (*All laugh. Curtain*)

*   *   *   *   *

SCENE 3

SETTING: *Inside Hare's house.*

AT RISE: HARE *and* GRASSHOPPER *enter.*

HARE: Brr. You know, it's getting cold out there. And I saw a few snowflakes.

GRASSHOPPER: Yes, who would have thought that it would snow so early this year?

HARE: I'll just find my warm scarf, and then get out there and win this race. Then I can come back and take my afternoon nap. I'm feeling tired.

GRASSHOPPER: The carrot pie over there looks delicious. I wish I had stored away food like that smart little ant. Now

I'm really hungry, and I won't be able to find any food if it starts to snow a lot.

HARE: Too bad. But don't expect *me* to give you any food — unless you pay for it, of course.

GRASSHOPPER: I don't have any money, but I could play you a tune on my violin in exchange for a piece of that carrot pie.

HARE: Well-l-l. Maybe half a piece.

GRASSHOPPER: It's a deal. (*Plays a tune on violin. See Production Notes.*)

HARE: Oh, my, that was pretty...so soothing...and relaxing....(*Snores*)

GRASSHOPPER: Hmm, he fell asleep. I'd better wake him up for that race...No, on second thought, I'll just sit here and enjoy this carrot pie. (*Eating*) Yum, yum. Besides, when he wakes up, I'll have to go out into all that cold and snow, and it's so nice and warm and cozy here. So nice ... and ... warm ... (*Snores. Curtain*)

*   *   *   *   *

SCENE 4

SETTING: *A hill with the finish line at bottom. Everything is covered with snow.*

AT RISE: LION *is at finish line.*

LION: Come on, Tortoise, you can make it. Hurry! (TORTOISE *enters at top of hill.*)

TORTOISE: Oh, dear me. I don't know if I can keep up this fast pace. I'm 200 years old, you know.

LION: You can do it. Hurry! (MOUSE *enters*)

MOUSE: Yes, just keep going — you'll make it.

TORTOISE: Maybe I had better rest a moment.

LION: No, don't stop. Keep walking.

MOUSE: You have to teach that Hare a lesson.

HARE (*Appearing*): Did someone mention my name? It's a good thing I woke up when I did. It looks as though you almost won, chum. Too bad. Better luck next race. See you at the finish line.

MOUSE: Do something, Tortoise. He'll win.

TORTOISE: I know! Nothing was said about what kind of race this was, so — tip me over.

MOUSE: Tip you over?

TORTOISE: Yes, hurry.

MOUSE: Very well. (*Tips* TORTOISE *over*)

TORTOISE: Now give me a push down the hill. (MOUSE *pushes* TORTOISE *and he slides down hill across finish line ahead of* HARE.)

MOUSE: Oh, it's a close one. Who won? Who won?

LION: The winner — is the Tortoise! The Tortoise won by a "hair"!

TORTOISE, LION *and* MOUSE: Hooray!

TORTOISE: Thanks for your help, Mouse. I couldn't have done it without you.

ALL (*Singing to tune of "Carnival of Venice"*):
>   It's nice to help each other
>   Whenever one's in need.
>   Be kind to one another,
>   And practice your good deed.

TORTOISE (*Singing*):
>   For if you help another
>   At work, at school, or play
>   The person that you aided
>   May help you, too, someday!

ALL: Hooray for the Tortoise!

TORTOISE: Hooray for love! (*Curtain*)

THE END

Production Notes

AESOP'S FABLES

Number of Puppets: 10 hand or rod puppets or marionettes.

Characters: 1 male or female for Narrator.

Playing Time: 15 minutes.

Description of Puppets: Aesop is an old man in white robes. Children wear simple robes in light colors. Animals may be realistic or may wear simple pieces of clothing — vest, top hat and tail coat for Grasshopper, skirt for Mouse, skirt and shawl for Ant, pants for Lion and Hare. Tortoise might wear a baseball cap.

Properties: Large bag, violin, net, scarf, carrot pie.

Setting: Scene 1: A path leading to a Greek village, which is visible in background. Scene 2: Outside Ant's warehouse — a mound of earth with an opening in it. There could be a sign reading: "Warehouse." Scene 3: Hare's house, with a window, a shelf with carrot pie and a bench. Scene 4: The finish line with a snow-covered hill.

Lighting: No special effects.

Sound: Recording of Greek dance music may be used.

Special Effects: When Grasshopper plays violin, for rod or hand puppet, put the violin and bow on a long stick and use like a rod puppet. For a marionette, violin is always attached to his hands. For the hill in the last scene, a triangular piece of cardboard is painted to look like a hill. For a rod or hand puppet show, it can be attached to the front of the stage, then flipped up at the right time. For a marionette show, attach it to the floor and raise when needed. When Tortoise slides down hill on ice, simply turn over the hand or rod puppet and slide it down the hill with your hand still inside. A marionette may be flipped over.

SNOW WHITE AND ROSE RED

Characters

NARRATOR
MOTHER
SNOW WHITE
ROSE RED
BEAR
PRINCE
DWARF
BIRD

SCENE 1

BEFORE RISE: NARRATOR *speaks to audience.*

NARRATOR: Once upon a time, there lived a poor widow with two young daughters. The girls were as fresh and lovely as the red and white flowers that bloomed in the enchanted forest near the inn which the widow ran. The mother named her lovely daughters Snow White and Rose Red, and they loved each other so dearly, they never wanted to be separated. One day, as the three were all sitting comfortably around the fire on their hearth — well, I won't tell you any more. Let's see what happened that day... (*Curtains open.*)

*   *   *

SETTING: *The interior of the inn. There is a table at center. A door is up left and a large fireplace is up right.*

AT RISE: MOTHER, SNOW WHITE *and* ROSE RED *are sitting beside fireplace.*

MOTHER: Oh, my! I'm afraid we aren't going to have much of a meal again today, girls. The snowdrifts have covered all the roads and no one has ridden past our inn for several weeks.

SNOW WHITE: Don't worry, Mother. We still have some bread and cheese left from last week.

ROSE RED: Yes, and there's that plum pie in the pantry.

MOTHER: I hoped we could share that plum pie with guests. It looks so delicious. Perhaps one of you girls could go out and get more firewood to keep us warm at least.

SNOW WHITE: I'll go look, Mother.

ROSE RED: No, we'll both go. You know how we hate to be separated, Mother. We shall never leave one another. Never, never, never.

MOTHER: Yes, dear, I know.

SNOW WHITE *and* ROSE RED (*Reciting*):
> We're Laurel and Hardy. We're pepper and salt.
> When one of us is tardy, we're both of us at fault.
> Some call us Punch and Judy. At work or at play
> We follow one another, like night follows day.
> We're mistletoe and holly, we're butter and bread.

SNOW WHITE: Snow White is what my name is.

ROSE RED: And I am Rose Red.

MOTHER (*Laughing*): Yes, yes. Now be off with you before it gets dark.

SNOW WHITE: The darkness doesn't frighten us, Mother!

ROSE RED: Not when we're together.

MOTHER: Surely you girls have a guardian angel watching over you. You're always so happy together and you've made this such a cheerful home, even though we have so little.

SNOW WHITE: What more could we want, Mother?

ROSE RED: We have each other, a roof over our heads, a warm fire in the fireplace, and all the flowers we can pick from the enchanted forest nearby.

MOTHER: True enough! Although I do worry about having enough food for you sometimes.

SNOW WHITE: Why, if we had too much to eat, you would have two fat, lazy daughters on your hands.

MOTHER (*Laughing*): Oh, tee-hee. (*Knock on door is heard.*) Quickly, girls. See who is at the door. Perhaps there is a tired traveler outside seeking shelter for the night. (*They go to door and open it.* BEAR *stands in doorway.*)

SNOW WHITE *and* ROSE RED (*Afraid*): Oh! (*Both run to* MOTHER. BEAR *enters.*)

BEAR: Please don't be afraid. I won't harm you. I am half-frozen and only wish to come in and warm myself by your fire.

MOTHER: Poor bear! I never saw a bear look more frozen than you. Come in and lie down by the fire, but be careful not to lie too close, or you might burn that pretty coat of yours.

BEAR: You are most kind. And who are these two charming girls?

MOTHER: My daughters. This is Snow White and this is Rose Red. Do not be afraid, girls. The bear will not harm you. Somehow I feel certain that he means well.

SNOW WHITE: We're not afraid, Mother.

ROSE RED: It was just a surprise to see a bear at the door.

SNOW WHITE: Here, let me wipe the snow off your coat. (*Does so*)

ROSE RED: And I will dry your feet. (*Does so*)

BEAR: You are all too kind. After I have warmed myself and rested a bit, perhaps you would allow me to repay your hospitality. I know several magic tricks I could perform for you.

SNOW WHITE: How exciting!

ROSE RED: I love magic!

SNOW WHITE: And can you sing, too?

ROSE RED: And dance?

SNOW WHITE: And tell us stories of the enchanted forest?

MOTHER: Girls! Can't you see how tired he looks? Snow White, you help me set the table, and Rose Red, you fetch the plum pie. Now we have a special guest with whom we can share the pie.

ROSE RED: Yes, Mother. (*She exits*)

BEAR: You mustn't go to all this trouble for me. I will be rested soon and will return to the forest.

MOTHER: I wouldn't hear of such a thing. You would surely freeze to death. You must stay here with us until spring.

SNOW WHITE: Oh, yes. Please do. (ROSE RED *returns with pie.*)

ROSE RED: Yes, please stay.

BEAR: Very well. But you must let me perform one of my tricks for you. Hide your eyes! (*They cover their eyes.*) You're not peeking?

MOTHER: No.

SNOW WHITE: Not I!

ROSE RED: Nor I!

BEAR: Then — Abba dabba dabba! (*Food appears on table. See Production Notes.*) You may look now.

SNOW WHITE: Oh, Mother. Look at all the food!

ROSE RED: Yes. And it smells good, too. Yum, yum.

MOTHER: How wonderful! Now we have company and enough food to get us through the winter. (SNOW WHITE *and* ROSE RED *dance with* BEAR. *Curtain*)

*   *   *   *   *

Scene 2

Before Rise: Narrator *speaks to audience.*

Narrator: And so the months passed happily. The two girls played with the bear, listened to his stories, and ate from a table that was always filled with food. Then, one day.... (*Curtains open.*)

*   *   *

Setting: *The magic forest. There is a log at one side and a rose bush nearby.*

At Rise: Bear *and* Snow White *and* Rose Red *are standing at edge of forest.*

Bear: It is time for me to leave you now. I must return to guard the treasures of the enchanted forest from the evil dwarfs.

Snow White: Oh, you mustn't go.

Rose Red: We would miss you so.

Bear: I'm afraid I must. You see, in the winter, when the ground is hard and covered with snow, the wicked dwarfs are obliged to stay in their lairs. But now, since spring has come and the sun has warmed the earth, the dwarfs roam about freely and steal all they can find. The treasure means nothing to me, but the dwarfs use it to wage war with each other and for other evil purposes. So you see, it is my duty to keep the treasure from them.

Snow White: We understand!

Rose Red: Farewell, then. But don't forget to return next winter. We shall miss you deeply.

Bear: Farewell. (Bear *leaves. As he goes, he brushes past rose bush*)

Snow White: Look, Rose Red. Did you notice as Bear passed that bush, a piece of his furry coat was pulled off?

ROSE RED: Yes. And I thought for a minute that I saw the glittering of gold through the hole in his coat.

SNOW WHITE: We must have been imagining things!

ROSE RED: Yes. How silly we are. But come. Let's see if we can find some mushrooms for supper.

SNOW WHITE: There are usually some under that old log.

ROSE RED: Oh! Did you see something white bobbing up and down behind this log?

SNOW WHITE: My! We really are seeing things today, aren't we?

DWARF (*Appearing from behind log*): Well, don't just stand there, you ninnies. Are you going to pass me by without offering any help?

ROSE RED: Look! It's a little man with a long white beard.

SNOW WHITE: And his beard seems to be caught in the log.

DWARF: Will you stop wagging those tongues of yours and get me out of here?

SNOW WHITE: What happened, little man?

DWARF: What happened? You blind goose! Stop rolling your eyes and use them. What do you think happened?

SNOW WHITE: Well, I . . .

DWARF: I was going to split this log for firewood. I drove the wedge in properly, but it was too smooth and flew out. The log snapped shut so suddenly that I couldn't draw out my bee-autiful white beard. So here it sticks, and so here stick I.

ROSE RED: Oh, how funny! (*Laughs*) Tee-hee!

DWARF: Don't you laugh, you stupid creatures. Ugh! How ugly you both are!

SNOW WHITE: Ugly, are we? Well, maybe we'll just wait for an apology before we give you our assistance.

DWARF: Oowwww — you horrid creatures!

ROSE RED: Horrid, did you call us? Well!

DWARF: All right, all right. Let's just say you're unusual.

SNOW WHITE: I guess that's a little better. Here, Rose Red, you pull that way, and I'll pull this way. (*They both pull on* DWARF.) Oh, dear! It's caught too tight.

ROSE RED: I'll run and get some help.

DWARF: You scatterbrains! Why call other people? There are already two of you, and that's too many for me. Can't you think of anything better?

SNOW WHITE: Don't be so impatient. Wait! I have an idea. (*She takes out scissors and cuts off the end of his beard. See Production Notes.*) There!

DWARF (*Rushing about*): Oh, oh, oh! Look what you've done! You stupid, stupid girls. You've cut off my bee-autiful beard. It will take me ten years to grow it back the way it was. Bad luck to you! (*Shaking fist*) Bad luck! Now go away and leave me alone so I can do some fishing. (*Picks up fishing pole and drops line at back of stage.*)

ROSE RED: Come on, Snow White. (*They start to leave.*) My, he looked so funny caught in that log.

SNOW WHITE (*Looking back at* DWARF): And look what he's doing now. What's left of his beard is getting tangled up in his fishing line. Careful, little man. If a fish bites, you'll fall into the water. (*Line is pulled from below, and* DWARF *is dragged along.*)

DWARF: Help! A stupid fish is pulling me into the water! Don't just stand there! Do something! (SNOW WHITE *and* ROSE RED *run to his side and hold him.*)

SNOW WHITE: I'll hold onto him and you try to untangle his beard and the line.

ROSE RED (*Working on line*): It certainly is a mess. Let's see. This knot belongs here and this string goes here. No, that's not right. Oh, it's no use. Only one thing left to do. Snow White, give me your scissors.

DWARF: Quick — my feet are getting wet!

SNOW WHITE (*Cutting off beard*): There! Now you're free!

DWARF: Oh, you donkey. You've done it again. You've cut off more of my bee-autiful beard! Look at me. I won't be able to face anyone for thirty years looking like this. The shame, the shame! (DWARF *picks up large filled sack from behind log and exits.*)

SNOW WHITE (*Laughing*): He'll probably make a lot of people happy by *not* facing them. Tee-hee.

ROSE RED (*Laughing*): Such a funny little man. And so rude.

SNOW WHITE: I wonder what he had in that big sack he was carrying?

ROSE RED: He certainly didn't offer to let us see, did he?

SNOW WHITE: Let's go home. I'm hungry after all that exercise.

ROSE RED: I wonder if there's any raisin beard — I mean, *bread* — left?

SNOW WHITE: If there isn't, we can go to town and buy some. (*They exit. Curtain*)

*   *   *   *   *

SCENE 3

SETTING: *Another part of the forest. Castle is visible above and through the trees.*

AT RISE: SNOW WHITE *and* ROSE RED *skip in, carrying a large shopping basket.*

SNOW WHITE *and* ROSE RED (*Chanting*):
> To town we go, to town we go
> To buy some ribbons and see a show.
> We'll look in windows and visit the wharf.
> We certainly hope, though,
> We don't meet that dwarf.

(*They laugh.*)

SNOW WHITE: Oh, Rose Red, look at that big bird circling overhead. What do you suppose he's looking for?

ROSE RED: Probably something to eat, or maybe some twigs for his nest.

SNOW WHITE: Look! He's swooping down on something!

DWARF (*Offstage*): Help! Help!

ROSE RED: Oh, not again.

DWARF (*Offstage*): Help! Save me! I'm a goner! (*Huge* BIRD *appears with* DWARF *in his claws.* DWARF *is carrying sack.*)

SNOW WHITE: It's that same little dwarf, Rose Red! Just look at his clipped beard.

ROSE RED: So it is! Well, I suppose we had better help.

SNOW WHITE: Shoo, shoo, you nasty old buzzard.

DWARF: Oh! He's pulling me away. Help! (BIRD *carries* DWARF *toward exit.*)

ROSE RED: Grab him, quickly! (SNOW WHITE *grabs him.*)

SNOW WHITE: I've got his foot.

ROSE RED: Oh, dear! Now the bird has his claws around what's left of his beard! Quick, Snow White, the scissors again.

DWARF: HELLLLLP! (SNOW WHITE *cuts the rest of the* DWARF'S *beard off*)

SNOW WHITE: There! (BIRD *drops* DWARF *and flies away.*)

BIRD: Caw... Caw... Caw... (*Exits*)

DWARF: Ooooooh! Now I have no beard at all. I'm bare! Oh, you meddling rubbish. Why didn't you cut off the bird's claws instead of my precious beard?

ROSE RED: Oh — we never thought of that.

DWARF (*Angry*): Dizzy, dizzy, dumb dumb.

SNOW WHITE: My, such language!

ROSE RED (*Picking up sack*): Here's your bag, little man. You must have dropped it.

DWARF: My bag — gimme! What are you trying to do, rob me?

ROSE RED: Careful. It's heavy! Oops! (DWARF *pulls it from her hand and he spills jewels all over a nearby rock formation. See Production Notes.*)

DWARF: Look what you've done. You've spilled it! Oh, my jewels... my precious jewels all over the place!

SNOW WHITE: Did you ever see such pretty colors?

ROSE RED: Where did you ever find such pretty stones?

DWARF: Don't just stand there gawking and gaping. Put them in my bag, idiots. Stupid creatures, ugly fools! (*He is quickly putting stones back into the bag. Girls help him. A loud growling noise is heard.*)

ROSE RED: What was that?

SNOW WHITE: Oh, I hope it wasn't thunder. (*She looks at the sky*)

DWARF: Oowwww — it's that horrid bear. Give me my bag so I can run...

ROSE RED (*Frightened*): Oh look, Snow White! (BEAR *enters and takes hold of* DWARF.)

DWARF: Spare me! Spare me, my dear lord bear. I will give you back all your treasures. Here — only spare my life. (*Hands him sack*) I am only a weak little fellow. Hardly a mouthful. Here, take these two wicked girls! They will make a nice meal for you! They are as fat as young lambs! Don't they look appetizing? Eat them! Eat them!

BEAR (*Growling*): Gr-r-r. (BEAR *picks up* DWARF *and throws him offstage.*)

DWARF (*Offstage*): Ahhhhhh! (*Girls back away from* BEAR)

BEAR: Don't go, Rose Red and Snow White. Fear not!

SNOW WHITE: That voice! It is *our* bear, Rose Red.

ROSE RED: Look, Snow White! (BEAR *changes into a hand-some* PRINCE *all dressed in gold. See Production Notes.*)

SNOW WHITE: Who are you? What have you done with our bear?

PRINCE: I was your bear, sweet Snow White.

ROSE RED: But who are you?

PRINCE: I am the King's son. I was enchanted by that wicked dwarf and had to wander around the forest for many years in the form of a bear until the dwarf's death freed me. He had stolen all of my father's treasures, but now he has received his well-deserved punishment.

SNOW WHITE: But what prevented you from slaying him sooner, dear Prince?

PRINCE: He had magical power in his beard, and only after his beard was completely cut off, did he lose his magic.

ROSE RED: Oh, my! No wonder he hated to part with his beard.

PRINCE: But I must return to the palace now and to my father and my twin brother, Prince Charming. I am sure that he will come to love you, Snow White, just as much as I now love Rose Red. Rose Red, say you'll be mine and come with me to the palace to be my wife.

ROSE RED: Oh yes. Yes, my sweet prince. I will gladly go with you. (*They start off*) Farewell, Snow White. Farewell!

SNOW WHITE: But Rose Red — you said that we'd never part. Oh, never mind — (ROSE RED *and* PRINCE *exit.* SNOW WHITE *sings a few bars of the song, "Someday, My Prince Will Come," then exits.*)

NARRATOR: But that's another story, children — and one I'm sure you all know well. (*Curtain*)

THE END

Production Notes

SNOW WHITE AND ROSE RED

Number of Puppets: 7 hand puppets.

Characters: 1 male or female for Narrator.

Playing Time: 15 minutes.

Description of Puppets: Snow White and Rose Red are sweet young girls. Each wears the appropriate color. Mother wears an apron over her dark dress and a baker's hat on her head. Bear, while large and bulky, should not look too fierce. Dwarf is short and dressed in dark green. He should look cross. His long white beard is in three sections, attached to each other and his face with velcro tape or large snaps. When it is "cut off" one section at a time is pulled off. Prince is a standard, handsome fairy-tale prince, dressed in gold. Bird may be flat cardboard for lightness.

Properties: Pie, large fake scissors, fishing pole with a line (a large fish could be attached to the end of the line), shopping basket, sack of jewels.

Setting: Scene 1: Interior of the Inn. Table is at center, with door up left and large fireplace up right. Scene 2: Edge of the magic forest, with a large log and a rose-bush. A stream may be indicated on one side. Scene 3: Another part of the forest, with castle visible through trees. There is a flat rock formation.

Lighting: No special effects.

Special Effects: Table should have a false flip-over top with all food attached. The false top is on the upstage side and is tipped up quickly to reveal food. When Bear turns into Prince, simply exchange one puppet for the other.

The flat rock in Scene 3 has a duplicate underneath with glass jewels attached. When bag of jewels spills, flip down the plain front rock to reveal jeweled duplicate. Formation may be flat cardboard.

RAPUNZEL'S TOWER

Characters

NARRATOR
NAOMI WOODCUTTER
ROGER WOODCUTTER
BABY RAPUNZEL, *their child*
WITCH
LUCIFER, *the dog*
RAPUNZEL, *at 21*
PRINCE

SCENE 1

SETTING: *In front of the Woodcutters' house.*
AT RISE: ROGER *is chopping wood.*

NARRATOR: There once was a poor woodcutter who lived
happily with his wife and baby in a little cottage at the
edge of the forest. (NAOMI *and* BABY RAPUNZEL *enter
and sit in front of house.*) One day. . . .
ROGER (*Chopping wood*): Good morning, Naomi. How's
our little baby, Rapunzel, today?
NAOMI: She's just as cute as ever. And she's beginning to
crawl. I just caught her crawling out of our garden into
the one next door.
ROGER: You had better be careful! That's where the old
witch lives.
NAOMI: I know. I'm taking Rapunzel indoors now. Breakfast is ready. Come in soon.

123

ROGER: I will, just as soon as I finish this pile of wood. (*Chops.* NAOMI *and* BABY *enter house.*) Such a good wife, and we are so happy to have such a sweet little child. No problem at all ... well, not yet. (LUCIFER *romps in and barks.*)

LUCIFER: Arf! Arf! (*Pants.* NAOMI *re-enters with* BABY.)

NAOMI: Look, Roger. What a sweet little dog.

ROGER: Come here, boy.

LUCIFER (*Panting*): Arf! Arf!

NAOMI: He's such a nice dog, and he'd be fine company for Rapunzel. And a good watchdog for us, too!

ROGER: Now, Naomi, remember that he probably belongs to somebody. Don't get too attached to him. (BABY *crawls up to* LUCIFER, *hugs him, pulls his ears, giggles and coos.*)

NAOMI: Look, Roger. How nicely they play together. We simply must keep him. I insist.

ROGER: Well, it goes against my better judgment, but if it will make you happy, my love ...

NAOMI: Oh, thank you, Roger.

ROGER: Come inside, pooch. We'll give you some breakfast.

LUCIFER: Arf! Arf! (*Jumps up and kisses* ROGER) Smack!

ROGER (*Laughing*): Get down! (*All laugh and exit into house. Curtain*)

*   *   *   *   *

SCENE 2

SETTING: *Witch's garden.*

AT RISE: WITCH *is in garden, with hoe, working on radish patch.*

NARRATOR: And so the little dog stayed with Roger and Naomi and Baby Rapunzel and became a loving member of the family. A few weeks passed, and then, one dark and gloomy afternoon . . .

WITCH: Oh, my, the garden is doing so nicely. (*Laughs gaily*) Look how big the cabbages are getting. The rhubarb is shooting up so high! And the radishes . . . ! Wait until Mama sees them! (*Laughs gleefully*) I hope no one comes into my garden and digs them up. The Woodcutter family next door lives awfully close, and with that baby, they probably eat a lot. Hm-m-m. Just so they keep out of my garden. (*Exits.* BABY RAPUNZEL *enters crawling. Giggling and cooing, she starts to pull up radishes. See Production Notes. She eats them with smacking sounds and an occasional burp. She also pulls up lettuce and scatters it about.*)

LUCIFER (*Running in*): Arf! Arf! (*He tries to pull* BABY *back, but she hits him with radish and continues pulling up vegetables.* LUCIFER *gives up and exits.*)

WITCH (*Entering*): Oh, no! Look what that child has done to my garden. Come with me, you naughty girl. (WITCH *picks up* BABY *and exits with* BABY *crying. Curtain*)

* * * * *

SCENE 3

SETTING: *The same as Scene 1.*
AT RISE: NAOMI *enters, then* WITCH *appears with* BABY.

WITCH: Yoo-hoo! Anybody home? Oh, there you are.
NAOMI: Yes? May I be of any help?
WITCH (*Sweetly*): Indeed you may, my dear. You can answer a small question I have, if you don't mind.

NAOMI: Well, if I can . . .

WITCH: Tell me, dearie (*Angrily*), does this belong to you? (*Holds up* BABY)

NAOMI: Oh! It's my baby. Where did you find her? She was here playing with the dog a minute ago.

WITCH: She was in my radish patch, that's where! (BABY *burps*) And she ate up twenty-one of my biggest, reddest radishes. I was saving them for a big radish pie for Mama's birthday. She will be three hundred next week. (*She cries*) Boo-hoo!

NAOMI: Don't cry. I'll be glad to pay for the radishes . . . but I'm afraid we don't have any money now. Perhaps in a few months.

WITCH: Months? *Months?* I want my radishes now. (*Cries again.*)

LUCIFER (*Appearing*): Arf! Arf!

NAOMI: Oh, here's our dog now. Bad dog! Why didn't you keep better watch over Rapunzel?

WITCH: *Your* dog? Why, that's *my* dog! First your daughter steals my radishes, and now I find it's you who have taken my dog!

NAOMI: But we didn't take him . . .

WITCH: Enough! Enough! Don't say another word, or I'll cast an evil spell on you. And I don't want to do that. I promised Mother I'd stop doing evil things.

NAOMI: Oh, dear!

WITCH: Come, Lucifer.

LUCIFER (*Growling*): Grrrr!

WITCH: Now see what you've done. You've turned my own dog against me. He doesn't want to come with me.

NAOMI: No. He wants to be with Rapunzel. He loves her. (BABY *pulls on* LUCIFER's *ears.*)

WITCH: Wants to be with Rapunzel, does he? Ah-ha! That's it. And fair payment, too. Since you took my dog, and then your daughter took my twenty-one radishes, I shall now take my dog, *and* your daughter ... and keep her for twenty-one years. One year for every radish!

NAOMI: Oh, you wouldn't do that!

ROGER (*Entering*): I overheard everything. You wouldn't do such a thing, would you?

WITCH: I'm within my rights.

NAOMI: You mean ... ?

ROGER: Yes, dear. What's right is right! Rapunzel must stay with the witch for twenty-one years. One year for every radish.

WITCH: Ha! A very sensible decision. I'm glad there are still some honest people left in the world.

NAOMI: But will we be able to visit Rapunzel?

WITCH: No! Not a chance. And don't try to sneak a visit when I'm not home, because I plan to hide her where I will be the only person she sees for twenty-one years. (*Laughs evilly*) Heh, heh, heh!

NAOMI: Oh, dear!

WITCH: So, until then ... bye-bye! Come, Rapunzel. Come, Lucifer. (*They exit.*)

NAOMI: What shall we do now? Oh, dear! Oh, dear!

ROGER: Now, now, Naomi. Everything will be all right. Besides, there's no way we can talk a witch out of doing what she pleases. At least we won't have to worry about the company Rapunzel keeps — she won't be having any for twenty-one years. (*They exit. Curtain*)

*   *   *   *   *

SCENE 4

SETTING: *The tower.*

AT RISE: RAPUNZEL, *now 21, is looking out tower window with her back to audience.* LUCIFER *is next to her.*

NARRATOR: Years passed, and Baby Rapunzel grew up into a lovely young lady. The witch kept her locked up inside the top of a tower somewhere deep in the forest. Rapunzel's only companion in all those twenty-one years was her faithful dog Lucifer . . .

RAPUNZEL (*Singing to the tune of "I'm Only a Bird in a Gilded Cage"*):

> I'm only a girl in a golden tower
> Alone, and so lonely, too.
> Won't someone please come, and take me away,
> Or I'll end up feeling so blue.
> (*She and* LUCIFER *face audience.*)
> Yes, I'm only a girl in a golden tower
> And I don't know what to do.
> I can't escape and no one knows
> Just where I am, do you?

(*Speaks*) Oh, Lucifer, I don't know what I'd do without you. (*She hugs dog and cries.*) Boo-hoo!

LUCIFER: Woof! Woof!

WITCH (*Offstage*): Rapunzel, Rapunzel, let down your golden hair.

RAPUNZEL: Oh, dear. It's the witch. And I haven't finished mending her broomstick. (*She drops her braids down outside window.*) Here you are, Witch. Ouch! Go gently! Owwww!

WITCH (*Appearing at window*): Well, dearie. Is my broomstick done? I'm tired of climbing your hair every day to get into this tower.

RAPUNZEL: No . . . er — I have a few more straws to fasten.

WITCH: Well, be quick. I must get to the market. They're having a sale on pumpkins.

RAPUNZEL (*Working on broom*): There! Finished! Here. (*Hands broom to* WITCH)

WITCH (*Inspecting broom*): Hm-m-m. They don't make them like they used to — cheap straw, poor quality wood. Oh, well, I must be off!

RAPUNZEL: Yes. You certainly are.

WITCH: What? What did you say?

RAPUNZEL: I said — er — oh, look at that star! (*Pointing out window*)

WITCH: Stars — already? I am late. I have an appointment at the beauty parlor at midnight. Bye-bye! (*She flies out window on broomstick.*)

RAPUNZEL: Alone again. (*Sighs*) At least she is company for me. Someone to talk to. (*Sings to tune of "Twinkle, Twinkle, Little Star"*)

> Little stars, my only friends
> Tell me where this huge world ends.
> From my tower way up high
> All I see is endless sky. (*She and* LUCIFER *look out window. Curtain*)

*   *   *   *   *

SCENE 5

SETTING: *The forest.*

AT RISE: PRINCE, *in his hunting garb, enters.*

PRINCE (*Singing to tune of "Twinkle, Twinkle, Little Star"*):

> Hunting, fishing, always play,
> Isn't there a place to stay?
> Where a maiden, young, can help
> Guide this lost and forlorn whelp.
> Forest show me where to find
> A wife that's just and good and kind.

Is there none that will appear
That I can call sweetie, dear?
(*He laughs*) Enough of this silly singing. I had better get
back to my hunting. Look! There's a rabbit. Maybe I can
catch him and keep him for a pet. (LUCIFER *runs in. He
barks and pants.*) Why, it's a doggie, right here in the
woods. Are you a pet of someone nearby?

LUCIFER (*Barking and nodding*): Woof! Woof!

PRINCE: Where does that someone live?   (LUCIFER *barks
again and points offstage.*)

WITCH (*Offstage*): Rapunzel! Rapunzel! Let down your
golden hair.

PRINCE: Listen! Someone is calling. Oh, I see! An old lady
is at the bottom of that golden tower. And she's climbing
up on two beautiful golden braids. Let's see what that's
all about. (PRINCE *and* LUCIFER *exit. Curtain*)

*   *   *   *   *

SCENE 6

SETTING: *The tower.*

AT RISE: RAPUNZEL *is at window, singing.*

RAPUNZEL (*Singing to tune of "Twinkle, Twinkle, Little
Star"*):
From my tower, way up high
All I see is endless sky.

PRINCE (*Offstage*): Rapunzel! Rapunzel! Let down your
golden hair.

RAPUNZEL: What's this? The witch returning so soon? She
must have forgotten something, or maybe her broomstick
conked out. Here, Witch! (*She puts her braids out the
window and* PRINCE *climbs them and appears at window.*) Oh! Who are you? *What* are you?

PRINCE: I am a prince, fair lady. I was riding through the forest when suddenly I saw an old lady shouting to Rapunzel. Two beautiful golden braids appeared from the tower window. After she climbed up them, I heard your beautiful voice, and I knew I had to see you.

RAPUNZEL: Oh, I am so happy you did. It is so lonely here with no one to talk with all day — every day.

PRINCE: Then why don't you leave?

RAPUNZEL: I can't. There are no stairs to or from the tower, and I can't climb down my own hair. And besides, I belong to the old witch until twenty-one years have passed.

PRINCE: Could I come to visit you every day? We could talk and I could tell you all about the outside world.

RAPUNZEL: Oh, would you? That would be wonderful. Only don't let the witch catch you. She is very protective and jealous.

PRINCE: Until tomorrow then. Farewell! (*He starts to climb out the window.*)

RAPUNZEL: Don't you think you'd better wait until I dangle my hair out the window?

PRINCE (*Looking below*): Oh, yes. I forgot.

RAPUNZEL (*Dropping hair out window*): There!

PRINCE (*Climbing down*): Farewell, again. (*He exits.*)

RAPUNZEL: Auf Wiedersehen! (*She exits.*)

NARRATOR: And so the Prince faithfully visited Rapunzel every day for many months and then one day . . .

WITCH (*Offstage*): Rapunzel! Rapunzel! Let down your golden hair.

RAPUNZEL (*Entering and going to window*): Right away, my prince. (*Lets her hair down*) What news have you brought me today?

WITCH (*Appearing*): News? Prince? So, you have been having visitors behind my back.

RAPUNZEL: Oh, dear, it's you. Where's your broom?

WITCH: It conked out. It was an old model anyhow. But don't change the subject. Who is this prince?

RAPUNZEL: He just happened by one day. Now he visits me daily, and I'm afraid I've fallen in love with him.

WITCH: Love! In love with a prince? Hmmmph! Such luck. The only person who ever visited me was a bill collector. Well . . . it must stop! We simply can't have it! You belong to me!

RAPUNZEL: If you're going to be like that, I suppose I'll have to tell you.

WITCH: Tell me what?

RAPUNZEL: My twenty-one years were up three months ago. I no longer belong to you.

WITCH: They are? You don't? Why didn't you say something three months ago?

RAPUNZEL: I have become very fond of you and I would miss your company.

WITCH: You have? You would?

RAPUNZEL: Yes, because I . . . love you.

WITCH: Awwwww!

RAPUNZEL: But I love the Prince also. And I wish to marry him.

WITCH: If it will make you happy. And besides, Mama has been feeling poorly lately. I should go stay with her.

PRINCE (*Offstage*): Rapunzel! Rapunzel! Let down your golden hair!

WITCH: Oh, oh! There's your boyfriend now.

RAPUNZEL: Here! (*Throws down her braids*) Climb up quickly!

PRINCE (*Appearing*): Rapunzel — who's this?

WITCH: Never mind. I was just leaving. And for a wedding present I'd like to leave you kids with this tower. Good apartments are hard to find nowadays. Bye-bye! (*She picks up her broom. To audience)* And you thought I was going to be nasty, didn't you? (*She laughs and flies off*)

PRINCE: Wedding? Did she say wedding?

RAPUNZEL: Yes, my prince.

PRINCE: Then, will you? I mean, are we going to . . . ?

RAPUNZEL: Yes, my prince.

PRINCE: Wow!

RAPUNZEL: Oh, dear!

PRINCE: What is it?

RAPUNZEL: If we live here in this tower, how will we get in and out?

PRINCE: Well, I've noticed that men are wearing their hair longer these days. If I let mine grow as long as yours, we can take turns going out.

RAPUNZEL: But we won't be able to go out together. And I'd like to introduce you to my parents, at least.

PRINCE: Maybe your parents would like to come and live with us.

RAPUNZEL: What a wonderful idea! I'm sure that Mother and Father would both enjoy letting their hair down, too. (*They laugh, then dance about.* LUCIFER *comes in and jumps about, barking.*)

NARRATOR: And so Rapunzel and the Prince were married, and they lived happily ever after in the tower with Rapunzel's long-lost mother and father. And everyone agreed to grow long hair and let it all hang out. (*Curtain*)

THE END

Production Notes

Rapunzel's Tower

Number of Puppets: 7 hand or rod puppets or marionettes.
Characters: 1 male or female for Narrator.
Playing Time: 15 minutes.
Description of Puppets: Roger and Naomi wear peasant costumes, as does the Witch, but she should wear dark colors and a tall hat with wide brim. Witch should not be too ugly or mean looking but funny. She might wear glasses. Lucifer is soft and cuddly and also funny looking. Baby wears a long white gown, and the grown-up Rapunzel is dressed in a plain, pretty gown. She has long blonde braids with bows at the ends. Prince wears hunting clothes.
Properties: Ax, bits of green paper for lettuce, hoe, broom.
Setting: Scenes 1 and 3: In front of Woodcutters' house. There is a pile of wood. Scene 2: The Witch's garden. There might be trees in the background and a suggestion of her house. There is a row of vegetables — cabbage, rhubarb, lettuce and radishes painted on a long flat. Scenes 4 and 6: The tower. There is a small window at back. There should be a hidden door at the base if you are using hand or rod puppets. Window should be open to the top if you are using marionettes. A small bed and chair might complete furnishings. Scene 5: The forest.
Lighting: No special effects.
Special Effects: When Baby pulls up radishes, one radish is sewn to her hand, so that it looks as if she's pulling up many.

THE ELEPHANT'S CHILD

Adapted from the story by Rudyard Kipling

Characters

NARRATOR
ELEPHANT'S CHILD
AUNTIE OSTRICH
UNCLE GIRAFFE
AUNTIE HIPPOPOTAMUS
UNCLE BABOON
KOLOKOLO BIRD
MR. BI-COLORED PYTHON ROCK SNAKE
CROCODILE

SCENE 1

SETTING: *A jungle.*
AT RISE: NARRATOR, *dressed as an Indian in turban and jacket, enters and bows.*

NARRATOR: In the high and far-off times, the elephant, O best beloved, had no trunk. He had only a blackish, bulgy nose, as big as a boot, that he could wiggle about from side to side. But he couldn't pick up objects with it. (ELEPHANT'S CHILD *enters, waving his short trunk about.*) But there was one elephant — a new elephant — an elephant's child — who was full of 'satiable curiosity, and that means he asked ever so many questions. And he lived in Africa, and he filled all Africa with his 'satiable questions. (NARRATOR *bows and leaves as* AUNTIE OSTRICH *enters.*)

ELEPHANT'S CHILD: Good morning, Auntie Ostrich.

OSTRICH: Good morning, Elephant's Child.

ELEPHANT'S CHILD: Ah, Auntie . . .

OSTRICH: Yes?

ELEPHANT'S CHILD: You have beautiful tail feathers.

OSTRICH: Thank you, Elephant's Child.

ELEPHANT'S CHILD: Will you show me how they move about?

OSTRICH: All righty. Like this? (*Shakes feathers and recites*)

> I am a lady ostrich. My plumes are pretty, and . . .
> When I am very frightened, I hide my head in sand.
> My wings are full and fluffy, and yet I heave a sigh—
> For I've a little secret — you see, I cannot fly.

(*She giggles.*)

ELEPHANT'S CHILD: But why do your tail feathers grow just so?

OSTRICH: Shame on you for asking such a question, young elephant. (OSTRICH *spanks* ELEPHANT'S CHILD.) Now, goodbye! (OSTRICH *exits.*)

ELEPHANT'S CHILD (*To himself*): Now what was wrong with asking her that? (UNCLE GIRAFFE *enters, nibbling at leaves on tall jungle trees.*) Good morning, Uncle Giraffe. What are you eating?

GIRAFFE: Leaves, young elephant.

ELEPHANT'S CHILD: You sure are tall, Uncle Giraffe.

GIRAFFE: And you're short, nephew!

ELEPHANT'S CHILD: Would you show me how high you can reach?

GIRAFFE: All righty. (*Stretches up tall and recites*)

> Uncle Giraffe is my name.

I seem gentle, but I'm not tame.
My neck is long — I reach so high
That pretty soon I'll touch the sky.
How was that?

ELEPHANT'S CHILD: Just fine. But, Uncle, what makes your fur so spotty?

GIRAFFE: You're never satisfied. I'll spot you, you bad boy! (GIRAFFE *spanks* ELEPHANT'S CHILD.)

ELEPHANT'S CHILD: Goodbye, Uncle. (GIRAFFE *exits.*) I sure am 'satiable! (AUNTIE HIPPOPOTAMUS *enters.*) Hello, Auntie Hippopotamus. (*She looks for him, peering about.*) I'm over here.

HIPPOPOTAMUS (*Peering right and left*): Over where? (ELEPHANT'S CHILD *changes his place.*)

ELEPHANT'S CHILD: Over here! (HIPPOPOTAMUS *looks in his direction, and he changes his place again.*)

HIPPOPOTAMUS: Over here?

ELEPHANT'S CHILD: No, over here.

HIPPOPOTAMUS (*Finding him at last*): Oh, here you are, my boy. Stand in one place. I have trouble seeing, you know.

ELEPHANT'S CHILD: I see well enough. Tell me 'bout you.

HIPPOPOTAMUS (*Reciting*):
I'm a lady hippopotamus.
I jump into the water,
And I hit the bottom, thus!
My eyes are very pretty,
And yet they are quite small.
If I don't look where I'm going,
I'm apt to take a fall.
People think I'm stout. I find
Size is just a state of mind.
My skin is tough and gray and thick,
My heart is large, just hear it tick.

(*She laughs.*) How do you like that?

ELEPHANT'S CHILD: It looks as if you're gaining weight, Auntie Hippopotamus.

HIPPOPOTAMUS: You insolent little elephant. I'm going to spank you for that. (*She spanks him.*) Now, be off with you. (*She exits.*)

ELEPHANT'S CHILD: Me and my 'satiable curiosity. (UNCLE BABOON *enters.*)

BABOON: Hello, there, youngster.

ELEPHANT'S CHILD: Uncle Baboon, won't you swing from the branches for me?

BABOON: Well, O.K.! (*Swings from branch*)

ELEPHANT'S CHILD (*Reciting*):

> My Uncle Baboon eats melons,
> He eats them with so much pride.
> The fruit is pink in color,
> The same as his backside.

BABOON: What did you say down there, Elephant's Child? (*He comes down.*)

ELEPHANT'S CHILD: Oh, nothing, nothing at all. But tell me, why do melons taste so?

BABOON: None of your business. (*Spanks him, and exits.*)

ELEPHANT'S CHILD: I'm afraid my questions and my 'satiable curiosity will get me into worse trouble yet. (*Exits. Curtain*)

*   *   *   *   *

SCENE 2

SETTING: *The same as Scene 1.*

AT RISE: KOLOKOLO BIRD *is sitting on a bush.* NARRATOR *enters.*

NARRATOR: And still the Elephant's Child was full of 'satiable curiosity. He asked questions about everything that he saw, or heard, or felt, or smelt, or touched, and all his

aunts and uncles spanked him. And still he was full of
'satiable curiosity. Then one morning, he came upon the
Kolokolo Bird, sitting in the middle of a wait-a-bit thorn
bush. (NARRATOR *exits.*)

KOLOKOLO BIRD (*Reciting*):
> Kolo — kolo — kolokolo!
> This song you must have heard.
> Kolo — kolo — kolokolo!
> It's from the Kolokolo Bird.

> Kolo — kolo — kolokolo!
> I sit among the thorn,
> Kolo — kolo — kolokolo!
> Since ever I was born!

ELEPHANT'S CHILD (*Entering*): Good morning, Kolokolo
Bird.

KOLOKOLO BIRD: Hello, there, Elephant's Child.

ELEPHANT'S CHILD: Kolokolo Bird, my father has spanked
me, my mother has spanked me, all my aunts and uncles
have spanked me for my 'satiable curiosity, and still I have
a new question. What does the crocodile have for dinner?

KOLOKOLO BIRD: Are you sure you want to know? The answer may lead you into deep trouble.

ELEPHANT'S CHILD: I mean to find out what the crocodile
has for dinner.

KOLOKOLO BIRD: You are a foolish little elephant, but if
you must know, go to the banks of the great gray-green
greasy Limpopo River, all set about with fever trees, and
you will find out.

ELEPHANT'S CHILD: Thank you, Kolokolo Bird, and thank
you for not spanking me. I'm on my way. Goodbye.

KOLOKOLO BIRD: Goodbye and take care . . . (ELEPHANT'S
CHILD *exits. Curtain*)

*   *   *   *   *

SCENE 3

SETTING: *The banks of the great gray-green, greasy Limpopo River. It is dark and foreboding.*
AT RISE: MR. BI-COLORED PYTHON ROCK SNAKE *is onstage.* CROCODILE *is lying down asleep and looking like a
log on the river bank.* NARRATOR *enters.*

NARRATOR: And so the Elephant's Child left his part of the
jungle and walked on and on, walking east by north, till
at last he came to the banks of the great gray-green, greasy
Limpopo River, all set about with fever trees — precisely
as the Kolokolo Bird had said. (ELEPHANT'S CHILD *enters.*) Now you must know and understand, O best beloved, that until that very week and day and hour and
minute, this 'satiable Elephant's Child had never seen a
crocodile, and did not know what one was like. It was all
his 'satiable curiosity. (NARRATOR *exits.*)
ELEPHANT'S CHILD (*To* SNAKE): 'Scuse me, but have you
seen such a thing as a crocodile in these promiscuous
parts?
SNAKE: Me? A Bi-Colored Python Rock Snake? Have I
seen a crocodile? What will you ask me next?
ELEPHANT'S CHILD: 'Scuse me, but could you kindly tell
me what he has for dinner?
SNAKE: Shame on you for asking a perfect stranger such a
question. (*He uncurls and spanks* ELEPHANT'S CHILD.)
ELEPHANT'S CHILD: That is odd, because my father and my
mother and all my aunts and uncles spanked me for my
'satiable curiosity. I suppose this is the same thing.
Goodbye, Mr. Bi-Colored Python Rock Snake. (ELE-
PHANT'S CHILD *walks on* CROCODILE.) Is this a log I'm
standing on? I'd better step off. (CROCODILE *raises his
head.*) Oh! 'Scuse me, but do you happen to have seen a
crocodile in these promiscuous parts? (*He backs up.*)

CROCODILE (*Speaking in an oily manner*): Come here, little one. Why do you ask such a question?

ELEPHANT'S CHILD: 'Scuse me, but I don't want to be spanked any more.

CROCODILE: Come hither, little one, for I am the Crocodile, and I'm weeping crocodile tears to prove that it is quite true.

ELEPHANT'S CHILD: You are the very person I have been looking for all these long days. (*Approaches* CROCODILE) Will you please tell me what you have for dinner?

CROCODILE: Come here, little one, and I'll whisper it to you.

ELEPHANT'S CHILD: All right, Mr. Crocodile. Like this? (*Comes close to* CROCODILE)

CROCODILE: That's just fine. Just . . . like . . . that! (CROCO-DILE *clamps down on* ELEPHANT'S CHILD'S *nose.*)

ELEPHANT'S CHILD: Ouch! Oh-h-h!

CROCODILE (*Still holding on*): I think . . . I think today I'll begin my dinner with the Elephant's Child.

ELEPHANT'S CHILD: Let go . . . . You are hurting me! (*Snake hurries over.*)

SNAKE (*To* ELEPHANT'S CHILD): My young friend, if you do not now, immediately and instantly, pull as hard as ever you can, it is my opinion that your acquaintance in the large-pattern leather ulster, the Crocodile, will jerk you into yonder limpid stream before you can say Jack Robinson. . . .

ELEPHANT'S CHILD (*Pulling backwards*): I'b pullig. (*His nose begins to stretch longer and longer.*)

CROCODILE (*Pulling in opposite direction*): You be quiet, Bi-Colored Python Rock Snake. (ELEPHANT'S CHILD'S *nose keeps stretching.*)

ELEPHANT'S CHILD: Oh, by doze! Bi-Colored Pythod Rog Snag . . . by legs are slibbig.

SNAKE: Rash and inexperienced traveler, we will seriously devote ourselves to a little high tension, because if we do not, it is my impression that yonder self-propelling man-of-war with the armor-plated upper deck, the Crocodile, will permanently vitiate your future career. (SNAKE *takes hold of* ELEPHANT'S CHILD'S *tail and pulls.* NARRATOR *enters while pulling contest continues.*)

NARRATOR: And so the Bi-Colored Python Rock Snake pulled, and the Elephant's Child pulled, and the Crocodile pulled, but the Elephant's Child and the Bi-Colored Python Rock Snake pulled harder, and at last the Crocodile let go of the Elephant's Child's nose with a plop (*Loud plop sound is heard, and* CROCODILE *sinks into river.*) that you could hear all up and down the great gray-green greasy Limpopo River. (ELEPHANT'S CHILD *hangs his new long trunk over the edge of the stage.*)

ELEPHANT'S CHILD: Thank you, Mr. Bi-Colored Python Rock Snake.

SNAKE: Why are you hanging your nose in the water?

ELEPHANT'S CHILD: 'Scuse me, but my nose is badly out of shape, and I'm waiting for it to shrink.

SNAKE: Then you will wait a long time. Some people do not know what is good for them. (SNAKE *slinks off.*)

NARRATOR (*Entering*): The Elephant's Child sat there at the edge of the river for three days, waiting for his nose to shrink, but it never grew any shorter, and besides it made him squint. For, O best beloved, you will see and understand that the Crocodile had pulled it out into a really truly trunk, the same as all elephants have today. (NARRATOR *bows and exits.* ELEPHANT'S CHILD *gets up and slowly exits, swinging his new long trunk from side to side. Curtain*)

THE END

Production Notes

THE ELEPHANT'S CHILD

Number of Puppets: 9 hand or rod puppets or marionettes. If desired, Narrator may be an actor.

Playing Time: 15 minutes.

Description of Puppets: Narrator is dressed as an Indian in turban and Nehru jacket. Crocodile and Snake should be Muppet-type "mouth" puppets, so they can hold onto elephant's trunk and tail. The other animals may be stylized and fanciful. To make the Elephant's Child's nose, use a small Slinky (the toy made of a loose coiled spring), covered with a lightweight jersey material. Use Velcro tape or two large snaps to hold the closed spring in place until it is stretched at the end of the play. Then open snaps or tape and spring will pull out as if the nose is stretching.

Properties: None required.

Setting: Simple jungle background. There should be a bush or tree with branches for Bird to sit on and Baboon to swing from. The first two scenes should be in light greens, and the river scene in dark grays and greens.

Lighting: No special effects.

Sound: Recording of Indian or African music might be used.

THREE BILLY GOATS GRUFF

Characters

GRANNIE OLSEN
BILLY
GRETA
LITTLE GOAT
MIDDLE GOAT
BIG GOAT
TROLL

SCENE 1

SETTING: *Grannie Olsen's little house, in Norway.*

AT RISE: GRANNIE *is rocking in her rocking chair, knitting.* BILLY *and* GRETA *are building a bridge from wooden blocks.* GRETA *has a toy goat.*

BILLY (*Grabbing the goat*): Give me that goat. It's mine. I want to make him walk across the bridge. Greta, let go!

GRETA (*Pulling goat back*): But I only want to... (BILLY *pulls goat*)

BILLY: I don't care. It's mine, and I can do what I want with it.

GRETA: Then you can't play with my blocks.

BILLY: Here.... Take your old blocks. (*Knocks over bridge*)

GRETA: All right for you, Billy.

GRANNIE: Now, children, don't be so greedy. It's not nice. Come, sit here next to Grannie Olsen, and I'll tell you a story about sharing and being kind to each other.

145

GRETA: Oh, goody. I love stories.

BILLY: Well, O.K. Just so it isn't mushy.

GRANNIE: Oh, it's exciting. You see, it's about goats and bridges and...a troll!

GRETA *and* BILLY: Oh-h-h! Tell us, please.

BILLY: Trolls are ugly and fierce and mean.

GRANNIE: This troll was all of those things, but the Three Billy Goats Gruff taught him a lesson. Now, sit here by my side and I'll begin my story, and when I'm through, it's off to bed for both of you. Once upon a time... (*Curtain*)

*　　*　　*　　*　　*

SCENE 2

BEFORE RISE: GRANNIE *speaks offstage, or in front of curtain, while stage is being set up.*

GRANNIE: Once upon a time, there lived a family of three goats on the side of a peaceful hill. Every day when the sun became too hot they would move across a little bridge to another hill where it was cooler and shadier. But one day...(*Curtains open*)

*　　*　　*

SETTING: *Two hills connected by a bridge at center. A shady tree is on one side. The other side is sunny.*

AT RISE: LITTLE GOAT *is grazing on the sunny side.*

LITTLE GOAT (*Singing to tune of "Over the River"*):
Over the river, across the bridge,
To the shady side I go.
I know the way,

'Cause that's where I play
When the sun's too hot, you know.
Over the river, across the bridge,
That's where I'll play all day.
My brothers will come
And join in the fun
Till the sunshine goes away.

Oh, my. The sun is very hot today. I can't wait to get to my favorite shady spot on the other side of the bridge. (*Walks across bridge. Sounds of clip, clop, clip, clop are heard.* TROLL *appears under bridge as* LITTLE GOAT *gets halfway across.*)

TROLL: Hey — who's that on my roof?

LITTLE GOAT (*Stopping*): I beg your pardon?

TROLL: Can't you see where you're going? You're on my roof!

LITTLE GOAT: What do you mean, your roof?

TROLL: Goof? Who's a goof? I ought to eat you up for that.

LITTLE GOAT: For your information, this is a bridge.

TROLL: A what?

LITTLE GOAT (*Loudly*): A bridge!

TROLL: It is, is it? Well, whatever it is, it's my home now, and if you want to cross, you'll have to pay!

LITTLE GOAT: But, but...this is a free bridge — for everyone.

TROLL: Not anymore. Now it's a...*troll* bridge. (*Laughs*) Ha, ha, ha!

LITTLE GOAT: Oh, dear. I haven't any money with me.

TROLL: Honey? I don't want honey. I want gold. Or I'll eat you up.

LITTLE GOAT: Oh, please don't do that, Mr. Troll. My brother is coming soon, and he may have some gold to pay you.

TROLL: Oh, goody.

LITTLE GOAT: Besides, he's bigger and fatter than I am.

TROLL: You are awfully scrawny. Where is he, did you say?

LITTLE GOAT: He's up there on the sunny hill, near the big bush.

TROLL (*Looking*): What bush?

LITTLE GOAT: The one next to the big rock. (LITTLE GOAT *edges across bridge as* TROLL *looks.*)

TROLL: What rock?

LITTLE GOAT: Hmm.... I know he's up there.

TROLL: Oh, very well. I'll wait for him to go across. Hurry before I change my mind about you.

LITTLE GOAT: Oh, thank you, Mr. Troll. I'll hurry! (*Runs across bridge and off*)

TROLL: Worry? You don't have to worry. It's your brother who has to worry. (*Laughs and goes back under bridge. MIDDLE GOAT appears.*)

MIDDLE GOAT (*Singing or speaking*):
Some like the heat, but I'm no fool.
I like to go where it is cool.
I like to rest beneath a tree,
All alone or with company.
Clippety-clop, clippety-clop, clippety-clop....

Ah, that nice shady spot on the other side of the bridge looks so cool and refreshing. It will be a good spot for a nap this afternoon. (*Starts to cross bridge. Clip, clop, clip, clop sound is heard.*)

TROLL (*Appearing under bridge*): Hey! Stop! (MIDDLE GOAT *stops in middle of bridge*) Can't you see you're on private property?

MIDDLE GOAT: I am? Funny, I never noticed before. I thought it was free.

TROLL: Tea? Tea? Sorry, we don't serve refreshments, and you have to pay to cross, or else I get to eat you up.

MIDDLE GOAT: Some choice! But I'll tell you what I'm going to do, Mr. Troll.

TROLL: Yes?

MIDDLE GOAT: I'll pick a number from one to ten. If you can guess it, you get my money, and you can eat me up, too. If you don't guess it, I can cross the bridge for nothing.

TROLL: Oh, boy. I love games — but I get three guesses.

MIDDLE GOAT: Well...all right.

TROLL: Is it six?

MIDDLE GOAT: Nope.

TROLL: Three?

MIDDLE GOAT: Sorry.

TROLL: Ah-ha! It must be eight.

MIDDLE GOAT: Wrong again. But you were very close.

TROLL: Five?

MIDDLE GOAT: Well, don't feel too bad. (*Starts across bridge again*) My big brother will be coming by soon. He always crosses this bridge about this time each day. You'll like him. He's *really* big and fat.

TROLL: Oh, neato! How will I recognize him?

MIDDLE GOAT: By his big horns.

TROLL: Oh, how nice. I love tubas and trombones. They send me!

MIDDLE GOAT: These will send you, all right.

TROLL: I'll bet you didn't think I looked like the musical type.

MIDDLE GOAT: Oh, but you do. You really do.

TROLL: Aww.... Well, hurry across. I'll wait for your brother.

MIDDLE GOAT (*Crossing*): So long, and have a nice trip. (*Exits*)

TROLL: Now where did he get the idea I was going on a trip? Must be hard of hearing. Well, I'll just wait for that nice fat goat with his musical instruments. Nothing nicer than having music with your meals. (*Singing to tune of "Little Brown Jug"*)

Oh, I like music when I dine,
And tuba tunes are just divine.
It makes my meals digest just fine.
Oh, I like music when I dine.

(*Disappears under bridge.* BIG GOAT, *who has great curling horns on his head, enters.*)

BIG GOAT: Ho-hum. Now for a nice, cool nap on the other hill. (*Singing to the tune of "Pepsi-Cola Hits the Spot"*)

Ho-ho-hum, my work is done,
Time to leave the noonday sun,
And find a shady place to rest
Across the bridge, that's where it's best.

(*Starts across bridge.* TROLL *leaps up from under bridge and holds onto* BIG GOAT)

TROLL: Ah-ha! Gotcha! (*Suddenly noticing* GOAT's *size and horns*) Er...I mean, excuse me!

BIG GOAT (*Fiercely*): You got me what?

TROLL: Er — a free pass. That's it, a free pass over the bridge. You're the third goat to cross this bridge today, and you get a free pass.

BIG GOAT (*Butting* TROLL *with horns*): You had better get out of my way, or you'll be getting a free pass — with my horns.

TROLL: Yes, yes. By all means. Good day. (*Disappears*)

BIG GOAT (*Crossing bridge*): The things that litter the roads these days. Ho-hum. (*Exits*)

TROLL (*Reappearing*): Has he gone? Good. This certainly hasn't been my day. The moon must be in the wrong cycle. First I misplace my ear trumpet, then my glasses disappear, and now I have to go without lunch. What a price to pay, just for having a troll bridge.

LITTLE GOAT *and* MIDDLE GOAT (*Entering*): Yoo-hoo, Mr. Troll.

LITTLE GOAT: Did you lose this ear trumpet? (*Hands* TROLL *large ear trumpet*)

TROLL: Why, yes I did.

MIDDLE GOAT: And are these your spectacles? (*Hands glasses to him*) We found them over there by the well.

TROLL: My goodness, yes. Goodie. Now I can see again and hear again. And now, for lunch, I'm going to —

LITTLE GOAT (*Quickly*): Here, we picked some dandelion greens and some apples for your lunch.

TROLL: For me? Aww....

MIDDLE GOAT: And here are some wild strawberries for dessert.

TROLL: Oh, my. How kind. I promise never to charge anyone a toll to cross my bridge.

BIG GOAT (*Entering*): And you won't eat the pedestrians?

TROLL: No — never again. Unless maybe they jaywalk.

LITTLE GOAT:

> It's nice to be good neighbors,
> And cheer up someone sad.
> It's nice to help each other.
> It sure beats being bad.

MIDDLE GOAT:

> 'Cause when you help each other
> It brightens up the day.
> It cheers up those who need it
> And chases blues away.

BIG GOAT:

> So if you meet a person
> Who's sad or acting rough,
> Be kind, and try to help him —
> Don't be a goat that's gruff!

GOATS: This is the end, and no butts about it! (*Curtain*)

THE END

Production Notes

Three Billy Goats Gruff

Number of Puppets: 7 hand or rod puppets or marionettes.

Playing Time: 15 minutes.

Description of Puppets: Fairytale or costume books will give you ideas for Norwegian costumes for Grannie and children. Troll might also be dressed this way — but he is not too neat and is quite ugly and funny looking. The three goats are small, medium and large sized.

Properties: Knitting, small toy bridge (should only look as if it were made of blocks; it is really one piece), toy goat, ear trumpet, eyeglasses, dandelion greens, apples, strawberries.

Setting: Scene 1: Grannie Olsen's little house in Norway. There is a rocking chair. Scene 2: Two hills, connected by bridge at center. For a hand or rod puppet show, this can be a cut-out attached to front of stage. One hill has a tree and is shady, the other is sunny.

Lighting: No special effects.

Sound: "Morning" and "In the Hall of the Mountain King" from Grieg's *Peer Gynt Suite* might be used.

BEAUTY AND THE BEAST

Characters

NARRATOR, *boy or girl*
PRINCE LEON
THE BEAST
OWL
ENCHANTRESS
FATHER
BEAUTY
BRENDA }
AGATHA } *her sisters*
FOREST ANIMALS

SCENE 1

BEFORE RISE: NARRATOR *addresses audience.*
NARRATOR: Here is the story of Beauty and the Beast —
where a lesson is learned in a most unusual way. There
was once a proud and selfish young prince, who liked to
hunt in his woods. (*Curtain opens.*)

*   *   *

SETTING: *A dark forest backdrop, with one large tree at
one side and bush with one rose on the other side.*
AT RISE: FOREST ANIMALS (*rabbits, squirrels, etc.*) *run
about.* OWL *flies in.*

OWL: Whooo! Whooo! You had better hop out of this part
of the forest. Prince Leon hunts in these woods, and your

153

life isn't worth much jumping about here. Whooo! Whooo! Here he comes now...scoot! (ANIMALS *run off, as a shot is heard.*)

PRINCE (*Entering*): Missed him.

OWL (*Flying about*): Whooo! Whooo!

PRINCE: Oh, be quiet, Owl. Don't bother me with your hooting. This forest belongs to me, and I'll hunt any animal I wish.

ENCHANTRESS (*Appearing*): And any forest spirit as well?

PRINCE (*Crossly*): Who are you?

ENCHANTRESS: Forest Enchantress supreme....

PRINCE: You're in my forest. *I'm* supreme here, and I'll ask you to leave right away.

ENCHANTRESS: It seems you should be taught a lesson — to be humble, young man. The life of a lonely animal would teach you a good lesson.

PRINCE: Forest enchantress, indeed!

ENCHANTRESS (*Chanting*):

> Prince Leon, selfish and vain,
> Who knows nothing of humility and pain —
> Turn into a beast, ugly but pure,
> And remain as such, till love does cure....

(PRINCE *turns into* BEAST. *See Production Notes.*) Now, my proud beast, hunt no more my beautiful forest creatures. And let no one touch my trees or flowers or else he will die. Goodbye, Prince Leon. (*She exits. Sound of a rainstorm is heard suddenly, and* BEAST *hides behind tree.* FATHER *enters, with large bag.*)

FATHER: What a dark, sinister glen this is! I've lost my way to the main road. (*Looks around*) I hope I find my way home soon. This storm is getting worse. (*Goes to tree*) There seems to be some protection under this tree. (*Sound of rain decreases.*) Let's see now. (*Looks into bag*) I have all my gifts for my daughters. A scarf for

Agatha. A bracelet for Brenda. But poor Beauty. She wanted a single rose, but there was none to be had, with winter so near... (*Rain stops*) Oh! A bush with *one* rose left. (*Goes to bush*) Beauty will be pleased. She is such a good child, and I especially want to make her happy. (*He plucks rose.*) For Beauty! (BEAST *appears suddenly.*)

BEAST: Who dares to pick the Enchantress's rose?

FATHER (*Frightened*): A terrible beast! Help!

BEAST (*Approaching him*): There's no one to help you here. This is my forest.

FATHER: I didn't know. What can I do to make amends?

BEAST: Send me one of your daughters, or else you die!

FATHER (*Pleading*): But I love all my daughters...

BEAST: Just until I learn what love is...or else you die.

FATHER: You have much to learn. I do not wish to die, so I'll send a daughter. Goodbye, Beast. (*They exit on opposite sides.* OWL *flies in.*)

OWL: Whooo! A lesson to be learned. (*Curtain*)

*   *   *   *   *

SCENE 2

TIME: *A short time later.*

SETTING: *Beauty's cottage. There are a large chest, table and chairs.*

AT RISE: FATHER *enters with bag.*

FATHER (*Calling*): Girls! Agatha, Brenda, Beauty. I'm home. (AGATHA, BRENDA *and* BEAUTY *run in.*)

AGATHA: What do you have for us?

BRENDA: Did you bring my bracelet?

BEAUTY: Welcome home, Papa! Did you have a nice trip?

FATHER: Yes. I sold all my goods and bought what you asked for. (*Takes blue scarf out of bag*) Your scarf, Agatha.

AGATHA (*Taking scarf*): It's not the right shade of blue. And it's too short.

FATHER: That's all I could afford. Brenda, your bracelet. (*Takes bracelet from bag and hands it to* BRENDA)

BRENDA: Hm-m-m. It looks like glass to me.

FATHER: Here, Beauty, is your rose. (*Takes rose from bag*)

BEAUTY (*Taking it*): It's beautiful, Father. Thank you.

AGATHA: A rose? It will just wither and die.

BRENDA: Much good it will do you.

BEAUTY: But where did you find a rose at this time of year?

FATHER (*Sadly*): Please don't ask me.

BEAUTY: Something is wrong. Tell us.

FATHER: I plucked the rose from a bush in an enchanted forest. Its keeper is an ugly Beast, who has threatened to kill me unless I send one of you to teach him about love. But I cannot send any of you away.

AGATHA: Well, I'm certainly not going to live in a spooky old forest.

BRENDA: I'm not going to care for an ugly Beast.

BEAUTY: I will go, Father. It was for me that you picked the rose.

FATHER: But, Beauty, I cannot let you go...

BEAUTY: Goodbye, Brenda. Goodbye, Agatha. Take care of Papa. Goodbye, Father. (*She exits. Curtain.*)

*   *   *   *   *

SCENE 3

TIME: *A short time later.*
SETTING: *The Beast's castle.*
AT RISE: BEAUTY *enters.*

BEAUTY: This is such a mysterious, spooky castle, but I — I won't be afraid.

OWL (*Flying in*): Whooo! Whooo!

BEAUTY (*Startled*): Oh-h-h!

OWL: Welcome — to the Beast's castle. Who are you?

BEAUTY: Hello, little Owl. I am Beauty, and I have been sent to care for the Beast.

OWL: He'll be here soooon...soooon.

BEAUTY: I'll be brave, even though my father says he is an ugly Beast.

OWL: Brave...brave...Whooo! Whooo! (*Flies off*)

BEAUTY: Perhaps I'll be happy here. At least I'll try.

BEAST (*Appearing*): Be happy?

BEAUTY (*Seeing him, turning away, frightened*): Oh-h-h.

BEAST: I shall do all in my power to make you happy. Please don't be afraid of me. You said you wouldn't be afraid. (*Pleading*) I need you.

BEAUTY (*Bravely*): How can I help you, Beast?

BEAST: You can brighten my days. You alone can save me from my fate.

BEAUTY: What can I do?

BEAST: You can teach me love. You can marry me.

BEAUTY: I will not be afraid of you, and I will be good to you, but I cannot marry you.

BEAST: We will have good times in my woods, and I'll show you my castle — and every fortnight, I will again ask you to marry me. Come... (*He leads her out.*)

NARRATOR (*Speaking from offstage or entering to address audience*): So Beauty and the Beast grew to know each other. A year passed, and the Beast began to learn humility, while Beauty grew to love the Beast. (BEAUTY *and* BEAST *enter. She is now dressed in magnificent gown and jewels.*)

BEAST: Beauty, once again I ask you to marry me.

BEAUTY: I've grown fond of you, but I still cannot marry you.

OWL (*Flying in*): Beauty! Beauty! Your father is very sick. Hurry home. Hurry home. (*Flies off*)

BEAUTY: Poor Papa. I must go to him. Please let me go, Beast. I've never asked for anything, but I'm needed at home.

BEAST: If you leave me, I shall die of loneliness.

BEAUTY: I'll hurry back to you. I'll remember you.

BEAST: All right, but just three days. No more, or I shall perish.

BEAUTY: I'll be back soon. Goodbye, dear Beast.

BEAST: Soon! (*They exit on opposite sides. Curtain*)

*   *   *   *   *

SCENE 4

BEFORE RISE: NARRATOR *speaks.*

NARRATOR: So Beauty rushed back to her sick father, and with her loving care he became well again. The days passed quickly, and all were happy — except Beauty's two greedy sisters... (*Curtain opens*)

*   *   *

SETTING: *The cottage. Chest filled with glittering dresses and jewels is open at one side.*

AT RISE: AGATHA *and* BRENDA *look through chest.*

BRENDA: Just look at the dresses Beauty brought with her...

AGATHA: And her jewels. Yet she wears her shabby rags here. Why she wears them after living in such finery, I'll never know.

BRENDA: She wants to keep them all to herself, that's why. She doesn't want us to see them. How can we get these lovely things away from her?

AGATHA: We'll just keep her here until we find a way. (BEAUTY, *in her old clothes, and* FATHER *enter.* AGATHA *quickly closes chest.*)

FATHER: I believe I'm much better now.

BEAUTY: Dear Father, I would not want anything to happen to you, but now that you are well, I must return to my Beast.

AGATHA (*Sweetly, pleading*): Please stay. Just a few days more.

BRENDA: The Beast will never miss you, and we've been so lonely without you.

FATHER: Yes, please stay a while longer.

BEAUTY: Well...maybe....

OWL (*Flying in*): Whooo! Whooo! Beauty! Three *weeks* have passed. The Beast is dying.

AGATHA: How did that owl get in here?

BRENDA: I'll get the broom.... (OWL *flies out.*)

BEAUTY: My Beast — dying? Has it been three weeks? Oh, I must go at once to my poor Beast.

FATHER: But we don't want to lose you.

AGATHA (*Aside*): Or the jewels.

BRENDA (*Aside*): Or the fine clothes.

BEAUTY: I must go to my Beast. Goodbye, Father. Goodbye, sisters.

FATHER: Goodbye, Beauty. (BEAUTY *rushes out.* FATHER *follows.*)

AGATHA: Ah-ha! She left her beautiful clothes behind.

BRENDA: And her jewels.

AGATHA: Let's get them.

BRENDA: Finders keepers. (*They open chest and pull out tattered rags and strings of onions and garlic.*)

AGATHA: The gowns are torn and falling apart.

BRENDA: The jewels have turned to garlic and onions!

BOTH: Oh, no! (*Curtain*)

* * * * *

Scene 5

Setting: *The Beast's garden.*

At Rise: Beast *is lying on ground, dying.* Enchantress *enters.*

Enchantress: Poor Prince Leon. I never meant for this to happen — from a handsome, vain prince to a lonely, dying Beast.

Beast (*Weakly*): It's too late. I found out what love is, when Beauty came, but too late...

Enchantress: My magical powers are not strong enough to save you from such human misery. Farewell ... and I am sorry for you. (*Exits*)

Beast: Beauty! Beauty! It's too late. (Beauty *rushes in.*)

Beauty: Beast, Beast — my Beast!

Beast (*Faintly*): Too late...too late.

Beauty: It's not too late. Ask me again!

Beast: Will you...will you be my wife?

Beauty: Yes, Beast. With all my strength and heart. (*She kisses his forehead.*)

Beast: Beauty.... (Beast *is transformed into* Prince, *and* Beauty *appears in her fine clothes. See Production Notes.*)

Beauty: It's impossible...you're a Prince!

Prince: I thought it was impossible to feel love — to know sharing and humility. But now your love has transformed me and changed me back into a Prince. Stay with me always, Beauty, and never leave my side again.

Beauty: I will be with you forever... my Beast! (*Curtain*)

THE END

Production Notes

BEAUTY AND THE BEAST

Number of Puppets: 9 hand or rod puppets or marionettes
(there should be 2 Beauty puppets: 1 in shabby clothes
and 1 in a rich dress and jewels); additional puppets for
Forest Animals.

Characters: 1 male or female for Narrator.

Playing Time: 15 minutes.

Description of Puppets: Beauty, sisters and Father wear
shabby clothes, with an elaborate dress for one Beauty
puppet, as described above. Enchantress wears beautiful
fanciful costume. Prince wears appropriate royal outfit;
Beast wears similar clothes, but with an ugly beast's head
(often a lion's head; see illustrations in a book of fairy
tales for ideas).

Properties: Bag containing blue scarf, bracelet, rose; chest
containing rich dress and jewels, ragged dress and
strings of onions and garlic.

Setting: Scene 1: Dark forest backdrop with large tree on
one side of stage, bush with one rose on the other; Scenes
2 and 4: Beauty's cottage, with chairs, table, and large
chest; Scene 3: Beast's castle; Scene 5: Beast's garden.

Special Effects: For the Beast's transformations, if using
marionettes, include a hillock in the setting behind
which the second marionette is hidden, and exchange
them. Hand or rod puppets simply disappear and are
replaced by second puppet. To change Beauty's dress at
end, have her back off stage (in surprise) and exchange
puppets. In the last scene, the garden might be dark,

with dying flowers, etc., with a second backdrop of a beautiful garden to drop into place after Beast turns into Prince. For a "gunshot" quickly strike a flat stick on table top or wooden floor. Storm can be a sound effects record of rain, or the puppeteers can make loud noises from offstage. Owl can be rod puppet attached to a light-colored stick and controlled from below, or on string and "flown" from above.

Lighting: No special effects.

Music: You might use Ravel's "Mother Goose Suite."

THE TALE OF PETER RABBIT

Adapted from the story by Beatrix Potter

Characters

NARRATOR
PETER RABBIT
FLOPSY
MOPSY
COTTONTAIL
MRS. RABBIT
MR. MCGREGOR
THREE SPARROWS
OLD MOUSE
WHITE CAT

SCENE 1

BEFORE RISE: NARRATOR *enters and speaks to audience.*

NARRATOR: Once upon a time, there were four little rabbits, and their names were Flopsy (FLOPSY *enters in front of curtain*), Mopsy (*Enters*), Cottontail (*Enters*) and Peter (*Enters*). They lived with their mother in a sand bank underneath the root of a very big fir tree. (*Curtain opens. Rabbits remain onstage.*)

*　　*　　*

SETTING: *Interior of Mrs. Rabbit's home.*

AT RISE: MRS. RABBIT *enters and speaks to others.*

MRS. RABBIT: Now, my dears, this morning you may go into the fields or down the lane, but don't go into Mr. McGregor's garden. Your father had an accident there. He was put in a pie by Mrs. McGregor.

FLOPSY: We are good little bunnies...

MOPSY: We are going down the lane...

COTTONTAIL: To gather blackberries.

MRS. RABBIT: Run along, now, and don't get into mischief. I am going out.

FLOPSY (*Handing her hat*): Here is your bonnet.

MOPSY (*Handing her basket*): And here is your basket...

COTTONTAIL (*Handing her umbrella*): And your umbrella.

MRS. RABBIT: I am off to the baker's. I'm going to buy a loaf of brown bread and five currant buns. Goodbye, children. Behave yourself, Peter.

ALL: Goodbye, Mama. (MRS. RABBIT *exits.*)

FLOPSY: Let's go to pick berries, Peter.

PETER: No! I'm going to Mr. McGregor's garden.

FLOPSY: Mama will be angry.

MOPSY: Shame on you.

COTTONTAIL: You'll be sorry. (PETER *runs off.*)

ALL: You'll be sorry, Peter! (*Curtain*)

*   *   *   *   *

SCENE 2

SETTING: *Mr. McGregor's garden. Some netting is at one side.*

AT RISE: PETER *enters and starts to nibble vegetables as* NARRATOR *speaks.*

NARRATOR: Peter, who *was* very naughty, ran straight away to Mr. McGregor's garden and squeezed under the gate.

PETER: Oh, boy. Do these vegetables look good! First I'll eat some lettuce. (*Nibbles*) Mm-m-m, good. And some French beans. (*Nibbles*) Yum, yum. And then I'll eat some radishes. (*Nibbles*) Oh-h-h, my tummy! I feel a little sick. I should be able to find some parsley to make me feel better. (*Exits.* MR. McGREGOR *enters on opposite side.*)

MR. McGREGOR: Another work day in my garden. I must pick some beans and radishes for Mrs. McGregor. I sure have a nice garden when those pesky rabbits aren't stealing from me. (*He looks over garden.*) What's this? My garden has been picked over. There has been a pesky rabbit here and just recently, too. I'll find him. (*Exits*)

PETER (*Entering and looking around*): Ah...now that I've had some parsley, my tummy feels much better. (PETER *starts to nibble, and backs across stage.* MR. McGREGOR *enters, walking backwards as if searching for* PETER. *They back into each other and turn.*)

MR. McGREGOR: What's this? Stop, thief! (MR. McGREGOR *chases* PETER *about stage and off, then onstage again for a chase back and forth.*) Stop, you pesky rabbit! Stop, thief! (*They exit.*)

NARRATOR: Peter was most dreadfully frightened. He rushed all over the garden, for he had forgotten the way back to the gate. He lost one of his shoes among the cabbages and the other shoe among the potatoes. (PETER *and* MR. McGREGOR *rush in, then out again.*) After losing his shoes, he ran on four legs, and went so fast that I think he might have gotten away altogether if he had not unfortunately run into a gooseberry net and gotten caught by the large buttons on his jacket. (PETER *runs in alone and runs into netting*) It was a blue jacket with brass buttons — quite new.

PETER: Oh, dear, I'm caught in this net. I'm lost for sure. (THREE SPARROWS *fly in.*)

SPARROWS: Poor Peter . . . we implore you . . . exert yourself. Pull, pull. Oh-oh, here comes Mr. McGregor. (*They fly away.*)

MR. MCGREGOR (*Entering*): Ah, there you are! Now I have you. (*He starts for* PETER, *and holds him by coat, but* PETER *pulls out of his coat and runs offstage.*) Come back, come back. Oh, well. I'll just use this little blue jacket and those little shoes for a scarecrow to frighten the blackbirds away. (PETER *runs across stage again and off.*) There's that rabbit again. He went into the tool shed. Now I have him! (*Exits. Curtain*)

*   *   *   *   *

SCENE 3

SETTING: *The tool shed. Large watering can and three potted geraniums are onstage.*

AT RISE: PETER *enters.*

PETER: Where can I hide? Ah! The watering can! (*He jumps inside watering can. With hollow voice*) Brrr! This would have been a beautiful place to hide if there weren't so much water in it.

MR. MCGREGOR (*Entering*): I'm quite sure he is somewhere in this tool shed. Perhaps he is hidden underneath a flower pot. (*Picks up each pot*) Not this one. Not under this. Not here either. Where can he be?

PETER (*Sneezing*): Kerchoo!

MR. MCGREGOR: Aha! He's in the watering can. (PETER *jumps out.*) Come back here! (PETER *knocks down geranium pots and runs offstage*). Now look what he's done. He's broken my potted geraniums. Oh, I'm tired of running after him. I think he's good and scared anyway. I'd better get back to work. (*He exits. Curtain.*)

* * * * *

SCENE 4

SETTING: *The same as Scene 2.*
AT RISE: PETER *runs in and sits down.*

NARRATOR: Peter sat down to rest. He was out of breath and trembling with fright, and he had not the least idea which way to go. Also, he was very damp from sitting in that watering can. (OLD MOUSE *enters with a pea in her mouth.*)

PETER: Dear little Mrs. Mouse, can you tell me the way to the gate?

NARRATOR: Unfortunately, Mrs. Mouse had in her mouth such a large pea she was taking to her family, that she couldn't answer.

MOUSE: Mmm-m-m. Mmmm.

PETER: You can't talk with your mouth full. Won't you please tell me the way?

MOUSE: Hm-m-m. M-m-m. (*Runs off*)

PETER (*Crying*): Now I'll never get out of the garden. (WHITE CAT *enters and sits at center.*)

CAT: Meow-w-w.

PETER: Maybe I can ask that pretty white cat the way out.

CAT: Meow-w-w. (*Swishes tail*)

PETER: No — it's best I don't speak to her. My cousin, Benjamin Bunny, told me all about cats.

CAT: Meow-w-w. (*Swishes tail again and exits*)

PETER (*Looking around*): Oh, there's the gate at last! (*Scratching noise is heard, and* MR. McGREGOR *backs in, hoeing.*) How can I get past Mr. McGregor to the gate? Oh, dear, I'll have to run for it. (PETER *runs by* MR. McGREGOR *and off.*)

MR. McGREGOR: Come back, you bad little rabbit! Come back here! (*Starts after him.*) Oh, he got under the gate. (*Rushes out. Curtain*)

NARRATOR: Peter never stopped running nor did he look behind him until he got home to the big fir tree.

*   *   *   *   *

SCENE 5

SETTING: *The same as Scene 1.*

AT RISE: MRS. RABBIT *is cooking at stove.* PETER *enters, panting.*

MRS. RABBIT: Peter, where have you been? What happened to your clothes? This is the second little jacket and pair of shoes you have lost in a fortnight.

PETER (*Weakly*): Mama, I don't feel very well. (*Moans*) Oh-h-h!

MRS. RABBIT: Well, you had better go right to bed. (PETER *lies down, and* MRS. RABBIT *covers him with coverlet.*) Now, lie there and be still. (*She gets out tea kettle and cup*) And here is some chamomile tea to make you feel better. "One tablespoonful to be taken at bedtime!" (FLOPSY, MOPSY *and* COTTONTAIL *run in.*)

ALL: We are home, Mama!

MRS. RABBIT: Get ready for supper. (*To* PETER) Flopsy, Mopsy and Cottontail are having bread, milk and blackberries for supper, but you shall have none at all. Now will you learn to be a good little rabbit, Peter?

Peter (*Groaning*): Yes, Mama. (*Others gather around* Mrs. Rabbit *as curtains close slowly*)

Narrator: We *hope* that Peter learned his lesson — what do you think?

THE END

Production Notes

THE TALE OF PETER RABBIT

Number of Puppets: 11 hand or rod puppets or marionettes.

Characters: 1 male or female for Narrator. If desired, Mr. McGregor could be an actor, with the rest of the cast puppets.

Playing Time: 15 minutes.

Description of Puppets: The Beatrix Potter illustrations will give you ideas for the puppets. Peter should have a blue jacket with big brass buttons. You may wish to redesign the show altogether, so use your imagination.

Properties: Bonnet, basket and umbrella, crepe paper lettuce and other vegetables, coverlet, tea kettle and cup, hoe.

Setting: Scenes 1 and 5: Interior of Mrs. Rabbit's home. Scenes 2 and 4: Mr. McGregor's garden. Lettuce, radishes, other vegetables may be growing in rows. Some netting is at one side — the gooseberry net. Scene 3: The tool shed. A large watering can, and three potted geraniums are onstage. Illustrations in the Beatrix Potter book will give you ideas for the setting.

Lighting: No special effects.

Sound: Simple piano music, perhaps "In a Country Garden," might be used.

ALADDIN, OR THE WONDERFUL LAMP

Characters

EVIL MAGICIAN
ALADDIN
PEDDLER
ALADDIN'S MOTHER
PRINCESS BUDDIR AL BUDDOOR
SULTAN
GENIE OF THE LAMP

SCENE 1

SETTING: *A street in Arabia, in front of Aladdin's house.*
AT RISE: EVIL MAGICIAN *is seated by a wall.*

PEDDLER (*Offstage*): Buy my baubles. Buy my wares. Who'll buy my strawberries?

MAGICIAN: All these poor peddlers and beggars scraping and bowing to each other. Ha! If they only knew of the riches in the magic cave...and of the wonderful lamp. But, alas, as clever and evil a magician as I am, I cannot enter the cave. Only an innocent youth may do so. Ah! To find a boy innocent enough to steal that magic lamp for me! (PEDDLER *enters, and* ALADDIN *comes in from the other side.*)

PEDDLER: Melons? Squash? Kumquats? Anyone to buy my wares? (ALADDIN *takes a melon and runs away.*) Come back here, thief! Thief! Bring that melon back! (MAGICIAN *stops* ALADDIN.)

ALADDIN: Let me go. Please! My mother and I are hungry.

171

PEDDLER: Give me back my melon.

MOTHER (*Entering*): Aladdin! What have you done? Shame! Please let my boy go. I am a poor widow, but Aladdin's a good boy. He's innocent. He did not mean any harm.

PEDDLER: *Thief!*

MAGICIAN: Let me pay for the melon.

MOTHER: Oh, sir...

MAGICIAN: 'Tis nothing. Here, peddler. A silver piece should do it. (*Hands him money*)

PEDDLER: The boy is still a thief!

MAGICIAN: Enough! Now be off. (PEDDLER *exits.*)

ALADDIN: Thank you, sir.

MOTHER: We are most grateful. Are you a stranger here?

MAGICIAN: Yes. I have come to find my nephew, my deceased brother's son. The boy's name is Aladdin and he lives with his mother somewhere on this street.

MOTHER: But he (*Indicates* ALADDIN) is the only boy here named Aladdin....

MAGICIAN (*Embracing them*): I knew it. My dear sister-in-law! My nephew! At last!

MOTHER: But my husband didn't have a brother...

MAGICIAN (*Interrupting*): I've found you at last. Please, nephew, you must help your old uncle find the jeweled caves. We will all be rich. Your mother will wear beautiful clothes and jewels and you will have plenty to eat.

MOTHER (*Aside*): Clothes? Jewels? (*To* MAGICIAN) Ah, you must be my husband's long-lost brother. Dear brother-in-law! Go with him, Aladdin. But come home soon.

ALADDIN: Goodbye, Mother. I'll return with armloads of jewels for you.

MOTHER: Goodbye, Aladdin. (ALADDIN *leaves with* MAGICIAN. *Curtain*)

* * * * *

SCENE 2

SETTING: *In front of walled-up cave. Cave should be able to open on cue.*
AT RISE: ALADDIN *and* MAGICIAN *enter.*

MAGICIAN: We go no farther. Here are the magic jeweled caves.
ALADDIN: But how do we get in?
MAGICIAN: You must say the magic words. Take this magic ring and read the inscription. It tells all. (ALADDIN *takes ring and reads.*)
ALADDIN:
>   Innocent lad, Aladdin I —
>   All evil curses, I defy.
>   Open caves, with jewels so rare.
>   A magic realm beyond compare. (*Cave opens with squeak.*) Let's go in now, Uncle.
MAGICIAN: No. You must go without me. Take all the jewels you can carry. And for me, bring only the little old lamp that sits at the base of the magic jewel tree.
ALADDIN: I'm on my way. (*He starts into cave.*)
MAGICIAN: Come right back.
ALADDIN: Right away, Uncle. (ALADDIN *exits into cave. Curtain*)

*   *   *   *   *

SCENE 3

SETTING: *Inside magic cave. An elaborate, jeweled tree is at center, with jewels and lamp at its base.*
AT RISE: ALADDIN *enters.*

ALADDIN (*Calling*): Uncle! It's dark in here. It's hard to see.

MAGICIAN (*Offstage*): Never mind. Don't dawdle. Do you see the jewel tree?

ALADDIN: Yes, there it is! It's beautiful!

MAGICIAN (*Offstage*): Pick up the lamp and hurry out.

ALADDIN: But I must pick up some jewels, too. (ALADDIN *picks up jewels and lamp.*)

MAGICIAN (*Offstage*): The time is short. Just hand me the lamp, and you can pick up all the jewels you want.

ALADDIN: I have the lamp and I'll bring it out with the jewels. Help me out, Uncle. (ALADDIN *goes to side.*)

MAGICIAN (*Offstage*): Give me the lamp first.

ALADDIN: I can't now, but I will as soon as I am outside.

MAGICIAN (*Offstage*): Unruly boy. Then stay in the caves — forever. (*Sound of rocks closing is heard.*)

ALADDIN: Uncle! Uncle! Here's the lamp. Oh, dear. The cave is shut. What will I do now? It won't do any good to cry or yell. No one can hear me. I'm all alone — trapped in these caves forever. What will happen to my poor mother? (*He sits down.*) I have these jewels for her and they won't do us any good. I wonder what that false uncle wanted with this lamp? It looks old and worn out. Perhaps if it were polished, it would look better. I'll just rub some of this grime away. (*He polishes lamp and* GENIE *appears*)

GENIE: What would you have, O Master? I am ready to obey you as your slave and the slave of all who may possess the magic lamp.

ALADDIN: Well, what do you know! No wonder he wanted this lamp. Genie of the Lamp! Take me and all these jewels home safely to my mother.

GENIE: At your command, O Master. (GENIE, ALADDIN, *lamp and jewels fly off. Curtain*)

*   *   *   *   *

SCENE 4

SETTING: *The street.*
AT RISE: ALADDIN *enters, carrying jewels and lamp.*

ALADDIN (*Calling*): Mother! Mother!
MOTHER (*Entering*): Ah, you're home, Aladdin.
ALADDIN: Look at all these jewels.
MOTHER: How marvelous. But where is your uncle?
ALADDIN: He was not my uncle, but an evil man who sealed me in the magic caves.
MOTHER: How did you get out?
ALADDIN: With the help of the magic lamp. The Genie of the Lamp is my slave and will do anything I ask him to. Let me show you. (ALADDIN *rubs the lamp and* GENIE *appears.*)
GENIE: What would you have, O Master?
MOTHER (*Frightened*): Praises be!
ALADDIN: Bring us food, for we are hungry!
GENIE: At your command. (*Food appears.*)
MOTHER: A miracle!
ALADDIN: And now, Genie, please take my mother, these jewels, and me to the Sultan's palace.
MOTHER: What are you saying, Aladdin?
ALADDIN: Please, Mother. I love the Princess Buddir al Buddoor and wish to marry her.
MOTHER: But we are in rags.
ALADDIN: That will be arranged. Genie! Off we go!
GENIE: Yes, O Master! (ALADDIN, MOTHER, GENIE *and jewels are whisked offstage. Curtain*)

*   *   *   *   *

Scene 5

SETTING: *The Sultan's throne room.*
AT RISE: SULTAN *is sitting on throne.* PRINCESS *enters.*

PRINCESS: Did you call for me, Father?

SULTAN: Dear Princess Buddir al Buddoor, it's high time for you to marry.

PRINCESS: Yes, dear Father. But there is no one I love.

SULTAN: Today we will receive princes for you to meet. There is one here already with his mother awaiting our interview. Show them in. (PRINCESS *walks to side of stage and brings in* MOTHER, *who is now beautifully dressed. She holds a platter of jewels.*)

PRINCESS: Good woman, please enter.

MOTHER: O Sultan, my son, Aladdin, wishes to present this small token as a gift to our great Sultan and ruler. He humbly wishes to be considered as the husband of the fair Princess.

SULTAN: Thank you, good woman. Have the Prince Aladdin come in. (MOTHER *exits.*) He must be a wealthy Prince to give such a great sum of jewels. (MOTHER *returns with* ALADDIN, *now dressed in elegant clothes.*)

ALADDIN: Thank you for receiving us, O great Sultan.

SULTAN: So you wish to marry my daughter. Do you have a palace fine enough for her?

ALADDIN: Look, my ruler! (*Back curtains are pulled aside and a beautiful jeweled palace appears.*)

SULTAN: Beautiful! More beautiful than my own.

PRINCESS: He is so handsome, Father.

SULTAN: You are, indeed, a wealthy Prince and will be a good provider for my daughter. (*To* PRINCESS) Go with him, Princess, and be happy. (SULTAN *and* PRINCESS *embrace, then* ALADDIN *and* PRINCESS *exit. Curtain*)

*   *   *   *   *

Scene 6

SETTING: *Aladdin's palace. There are many fancy lamps hanging from ceiling, and a fancy couch is at one side.*

AT RISE: ALADDIN, *carrying lamp, and* PRINCESS *enter.*

ALADDIN: And here we are, my sweet Princess Buddir al Buddoor.

PRINCESS: I am so happy. Your palace is beautiful.

ALADDIN: Now I must leave for a few hours to look after my mother's needs, but I will return to my bride's side in a short time.

PRINCESS: I shall wait for you forever, my Aladdin. (ALADDIN *puts down lamp and exits.*) He is such a good man. I am most fortunate.

MAGICIAN (*Offstage*): Lamps for sale! Lamps to trade! (MAGICIAN *enters with a basket of fancy lamps.*) Ah, Princess Buddir al Buddoor. Is the Prince at home?

PRINCESS: My husband, Prince Aladdin, is away.

MAGICIAN: But perhaps you have an old lamp you would like to trade for a new one?

PRINCESS: Not I!

MAGICIAN: Surely of all these lamps there is one that mars the beauty of this palace.

PRINCESS: Why, yes. There is an old one, but . . .

MAGICIAN: Exchange it for one of these beautiful new lamps. Won't Prince Aladdin be pleased by your cleverness?

PRINCESS: Yes. Oh, yes! They are handsome. Here is the old one. (*She gives him magic lamp.*) I'll take that golden one, there! (*He gives her new lamp.*)

MAGICIAN: Clever, indeed! Let us see if this is the right one. (*He rubs lamp and* GENIE *appears.*)

GENIE: I am the Genie of the Lamp.

PRINCESS: Oh!

GENIE: What would you have, O Master?

MAGICIAN: Ah ... it works! *It works!* (*Laughs evilly*)

PRINCESS: What have I done?

MAGICIAN: Genie of the Lamp, take this palace, Princess
  Buddir al Buddoor, and me to deepest Africa. (*To* PRIN-
  CESS) Now, Princess, you and this magic lamp are mine.

PRINCESS: Oh-h-h!

MAGICIAN (*Laughing evilly*): Ha, ha, ha. (*Curtain*)

*   *   *   *   *

SCENE 7

SETTING: *The same as Scene 6, except that an African jungle scene is visible at rear.*

AT RISE: MAGICIAN *and* PRINCESS *are on stage.*

MAGICIAN (*Evilly*): Happy, my little Princess? (*Laughs*)
  You'll never see your Aladdin again. We have been here
  in Africa for several months, and he has probably forgotten you by this time. Be satisfied with your lot.

PRINCESS: Never. Aladdin will search until he finds me.

MAGICIAN: He'll never find us here ... in the middle of
  Africa. (ALADDIN *appears at back and only* PRINCESS
  sees him.)

PRINCESS: Oh! (ALADDIN *hides behind curtain.*)

MAGICIAN: What is it? (*He looks around.*)

PRINCESS: Nothing. It's nothing.

MAGICIAN: Now to get my magic lamp. (*He exits.* ALADDIN
  appears again.)

PRINCESS: Aladdin, how did you find me?

ALADDIN: Sh-h-h. I asked the magic ring the evil magician
  gave me when we first met. We must be careful he doesn't
  know I am here. Take this goblet and see that he drinks

all of this potion. It will make him sleep and give us a chance to escape. (*He hands her goblet.*)

PRINCESS: All right. Oh, I hear him returning.

ALADDIN: Be sure he drinks it all.

PRINCESS: Yes, Aladdin. (ALADDIN *hides again.* MAGICIAN *enters with lamp.*)

MAGICIAN: Princess Buddir al Buddoor, what do you have there?

PRINCESS: I was about to quench my thirst from this hot African sun with a delicious drink of peach nectar.

MAGICIAN: Give that to me. I am the Master and should be satisfied first.

PRINCESS: But ...

MAGICIAN: Hush. The drink is mine. (*He takes it from her.*)

PRINCESS: Yes, O Master.

MAGICIAN (*Drinking down contents of goblet*): Mm-m-m! Delicious!

PRINCESS: Is there none left for me?

MAGICIAN: No! I was very thirsty. And now I am tired. The sun does make me sleepy as well. Ho-hum. (MAGICIAN *lies down on couch*) I'll just sleep a little while. (*He snores.*)

PRINCESS (*To* MAGICIAN): Master! Oh, *Master!* (*She sees that he is asleep, then runs to* ALADDIN's *hiding place.*) Aladdin! Quickly! (ALADDIN *appears.*) He sleeps. And here is your magic lamp. (*Hands it to him*) I am sorry.

ALADDIN: How could you have known? All is forgiven. But we must go back. And now for the lamp. (*He rubs it.*) Genie, appear!

GENIE (*Appearing*): I am the Genie of the ...

ALADDIN: Oh, let's get on with it.

GENIE: What will you have, young Master?

ALADDIN: Return the Princess, the palace and me back home.

PRINCESS: What will we do with the evil magician?

ALADDIN: I know. We'll put him into the magic cave. No. Better still — let's put him on the moon. Genie, take this evil man and fly him to the moon.

GENIE: Yes, Master. (GENIE *and the* MAGICIAN *fly off.*)

ALADDIN: Now we have sent him where he can do no more harm.

GENIE (*Returning*): It is done, Master.

ALADDIN: Good. And now for home!

GENIE: At your command, Aladdin. (GENIE, ALADDIN *and* PRINCESS *exit. Curtain*)

*   *   *   *   *

SCENE 8

SETTING: *The same as Scene 7, except jungle scene is removed.*

AT RISE: ALADDIN, PRINCESS *and* GENIE *enter from one side,* SULTAN *and* MOTHER *from other.*

MOTHER: Aladdin, where have you been?

SULTAN: And you, my daughter? We have been so worried since you vanished as if by magic.

ALADDIN: It's a long story, but we are home now, safe and happy.

PRINCESS: And never again will I trade my husband's lamp, and I will obey him always, may it do him ease. (*Curtain*)

THE END

Production Notes

Number of Puppets: 7 hand puppets.

Playing Time: 10 minutes.

Description of Puppets: Aladdin is dressed first in ragged clothes — baggy trousers, loose shirt and vest. He wears fez. Later he wears rich-looking pants, sash, jacket and turban. Mother first wears ragged dress and scarf. She later wears beautiful dress and scarf. Sultan, who may be fat, wears full pants and turban, jacket. Magician wears similar outfit. Princess wears colorful outfit, full pants, jeweled blouse and veil. Genie might have pointed ears and wear a full caftan or have a gauze body.

Properties: Fruit in basket, including melon, ring, coins, jewels and old lamp, tray of food, basket of fancy lamps, goblet.

Setting: Scenes 1 and 4: A street in Arabia. Scene 2: Outside magic cave. Exterior of cave may be painted on a curtain that parts so Aladdin can enter. Scene 3: Inside cave. A jeweled tree is at center. Scene 5: Sultan's palace. Throne may be represented by pile of cushions. Scenes 6, 7 and 8: Aladdin's palace. Fancy lamps hang from ceiling, and there is a couch on one side. There may be curtains and cushions in room. In scenes 6 and 8, outside of palace at back, towers and minarets are visible. In scene 7, an African jungle scene is visible.

Lighting: Scene 3 may be dim to indicate inside of cave.

Sound: Squeaking and crashing as cave opens and closes. Sound effects may be used when Genie appears.

THE NUTCRACKER PRINCE

Characters

KING WINTER
QUEEN BLANCHE
CLARA
CLARA'S MOTHER, *offstage voice*
PRINCE MARZIPAN (NUTCRACKER)
MOUSE KING
SUGAR PLUM FAIRY PRINCESS
SNOWFLAKES
CANDIES
OTHER DANCERS

SCENE 1

SETTING: *A dark sky with snowflakes.*
MUSIC: *Miniature Overture, Tchaikovsky's "Nutcracker Suite."*
AT RISE: KING WINTER *enters flying.*

KING WINTER (*Laughing*): Ho, ho, ho. Good Queen Blanche, come here! See what I see.
QUEEN BLANCHE (*Flying in*): What is it, King Winter?
KING: It seems that the silly Mouse King is making trouble for the Candy people of Sugar Plum Land.
QUEEN (*Concerned*): Oh, dear! And just before Christmas. Shame on him for stirring up trouble. You shouldn't laugh at a time like this. Should we stop him?

KING: What? And spoil the fun? Only if we are needed, Queen Blanche. The Candy people are as wise as they are sweet. But we will watch over them just in case. (*They fly off. Curtain*)

* * * * *

SCENE 2

SETTING: *Clara's living room, with small Christmas tree. Large window is at back, and toys are strewn about.*
AT RISE: CLARA *is playing with toys.*

CLARA'S MOTHER (*Offstage*): Clara! It's getting late. Put your new toys away and go to bed.
CLARA: Yes, Mother. (*To herself*) I wish I could stay up all night. Christmas is my favorite day of the year.
MOTHER (*Offstage*): Clara!
CLARA: I'm coming, Mother. (*To herself*) I think that of all the toys I got for Christmas, I like my nutcracker the best. (*Holds up small nutcracker shaped like man.*)
MOTHER (*Offstage*): Clara, I'll send that nutcracker back to Uncle Drosselmeyer if you don't mind me.
CLARA: I'm off to bed, Mama! (*To nutcracker*) Now, go to sleep, and we'll play in the morning. (*Puts down nutcracker and exits.*)

NARRATOR: So Clara went to bed, still with visions of sugar plums and nutcrackers in her head. (MOUSE KING *and* PRINCE MARZIPAN *enter fighting with swords.*)
MUSIC: *Mouse King Battle.*
NARRATOR: But what is this? Someone new has come on the scene. It is the hero, Prince Marzipan from Sugar Plum Land, and he is fighting the evil Mouse King.

PRINCE: Take that . . . and that, you evil sorcerer! You'll not get your grimy paws on my beautiful Sugar Plum Fairy Princess.

MOUSE KING (*Still fighting*): You are quite a swordsman, Prince Marzipan. And your spoken word is as strong as your sword arm.

PRINCE: Come on and fight!

MOUSE KING: Stand back! (*They stop fighting.*) This sword-play has gone on long enough. I shall turn you into that Nutcracker over there! Now your jaws will get a workout. Just you see.

PRINCE: You won't get away with this!

MOUSE KING: Oh, won't I? Into the nutcracker with you. (PRINCE *disappears.*) Ah-ha! Now back to Sugar Plum Land and the Princess. Yum, yum. (*Exits.* KING WINTER *and* QUEEN BLANCHE *fly by the large window and enter.*)

QUEEN: Oh, such an evil little mouse. We shouldn't allow this to happen. What should we do?

KING: I've awakened Clara with a strong gust of wind and snow on her window panes. Our Prince has certain elfin charms himself. Just watch and see. (*They exit.* CLARA *enters softly and looks about. She picks up small nutcracker.*)

CLARA: My beautiful nutcracker. I couldn't sleep thinking of you. A strong gust of wind and . . . (NUTCRACKER *appears.*)

NUTCRACKER: Please. You must help me.

CLARA: Nutcracker, are you talking? Who are you?

NUTCRACKER: I'm Prince Marzipan, trapped inside your Christmas toy. The evil Mouse King has put me inside it, and he has gone off to capture my Fairy Princess in Sugar Plum Land. Come with me!

CLARA: But how can I help? I'm only a little girl.

NUTCRACKER: I'm not sure, but come with me anyway. You will be back by morning.

CLARA: An adventure on Christmas! And I get to stay up all night, too. How exciting! (*They exit. Curtain*)

*   *   *   *   *

SCENE 3

SETTING: *Dark sky with snowflakes.*
MUSIC: *Dance of the Flutes.*
AT RISE: KING WINTER *and* QUEEN BLANCHE *fly in.*

QUEEN: Clara and the Nutcracker Prince are coming. Now, stop your snowing until they get safely to Sugar Plum Land.
KING (*Laughing*): Ho, ho! Snow! Snow! My snow will surround them and guide them. So dance, Snowflakes! Dance!
QUEEN: We must keep them in sight and protect them. (*They exit as* SNOWFLAKES *dance.*)
MUSIC: *Snowflake Waltz.*
CLARA (*Entering with* NUTCRACKER): Look at the beautiful snowflakes dancing. Let's watch.
NUTCRACKER (*Pulling her along*): No — we must save the Princess and my Candy people from the Mouse King. (*They exit. Curtain*)

*   *   *   *   *

SCENE 4

SETTING: *Sugar Plum Land, with buildings made of candy.*
AT RISE: CANDIES *enter, then* SUGAR PLUM FAIRY PRINCESS, *who dances.*
MUSIC: *Dance of the Sugar Plum Fairy.*

SUGAR PLUM FAIRY (*At end of dance*): Quickly, now, cinnamon stick, chocolate, and all the rest. Let's get ready for Prince Marzipan's return. It's Christmas night, and he will be back soon from his battle with the horrible Mouse King. (MOUSE KING *enters as they rush about.*)

MOUSE KING: Horrible, indeed! (*He grabs* SUGAR PLUM FAIRY. CANDIES *scream and run off.*)

SUGAR PLUM FAIRY: Let me go! Go away! What has happened to my Prince Marzipan?

MOUSE KING: I turned your precious prince into a nutcracker by my magic. (*Laughs*)

SUGAR PLUM FAIRY: Oh, sweet heavens!

MOUSE KING: And now you will be my bride, and all the Candies will be food for my mice.

SUGAR PLUM FAIRY: You cruel, ugly villain.

MOUSE KING: All I have to do is squeal on my silver horn, and all my companions will run here, scramble over everything, and gobble up Sugar Plum Land.

SUGAR PLUM FAIRY: No! Please don't! I'll go with you. Don't hurt my friends.

MOUSE KING: I'll count to three. (*Puts horn to mouth*) One! (*Breath*) Two! (*Breath*) Thr— (CLARA *and* NUTCRACKER *rush in and knock horn from* MOUSE KING'S *hand.*)

NUTCRACKER: Put down that villainous horn, Mouse King, and take up your sword.

SUGAR PLUM FAIRY: Who can this be?

MOUSE KING (*Taking out sword*): So we meet again. (SUGAR PLUM FAIRY *and* CLARA *stay at one side as* MOUSE KING *and* NUTCRACKER *fight.*)

NUTCRACKER: Our swords cross again.

MOUSE KING: Yes, but I have the upper hand. I will win this battle, and the Sugar Plum Fairy Princess will be mine. (MOUSE KING *drives* NUTCRACKER *to ground.*)

SUGAR PLUM FAIRY: Oh, what shall we do?

CLARA: I have an idea! I'll do what Mama does when mice get into the pantry. I'll just take off my shoe. (*She does so.*) Now, watch this. (CLARA *hits* MOUSE KING *with her shoe, and he falls to ground, dying.*)

MOUSE KING: Ah-h-h! (*Disappears*)

ALL: Hooray!

SUGAR PLUM FAIRY (*To* CLARA): Thank you very much, my dear. But who are you, and where did you both come from?

NUTCRACKER: This is Clara, and she is from Everland.

SUGAR PLUM FAIRY (*To* NUTCRACKER): I seem to recognize your voice, but I do not know your face.

CLARA: This is your Prince Marzipan. The Mouse King put a spell on him and placed him in my Christmas nutcracker.

NUTCRACKER: If you will open the nutcracker's mouth all the way, out I'll spring.

CLARA: All right. Here, Princess. You pull on one end of this stick, and I'll pull the other. (CLARA *and* SUGAR PLUM FAIRY *pull on the* NUTCRACKER'S *back stick and hold the jaw, and out pops* PRINCE. *See Production Notes.*)

ALL: Hooray!

PRINCE: That was a tight squeeze!

SUGAR PLUM FAIRY (*Embracing him*): My dear, sweet Prince Marzipan.

PRINCE (*To* CLARA): We thank you, dear Clara, for saving us from the Mouse King and his pack of mice.

SUGAR PLUM FAIRY: Please stay and celebrate Christmas with us.

CLARA: All right, but I must be home before dawn.

SUGAR PLUM FAIRY: You shall be. Now be seated over there, and the celebration will begin. (PRINCE, SUGAR

PLUM FAIRY *and* CLARA *exit as* DANCERS *enter and dancing begins. One or all of the following dances may be performed. See Production Notes.*)

MUSIC: *Chinese Dance, Russian Dance, Arabian Dance.*

KING WINTER (*Entering with* QUEEN BLANCHE *as dances conclude and stage is empty*): And so this is how Clara and the Candies of Sugar Plum Land spent their Christmas.

QUEEN BLANCHE: And we hope you spend as happy a one.

KING *and* QUEEN: Merry Christmas! (*They exit. Dance may end play. See Production Notes.*)

MUSIC: *Waltz of the Flowers.*

THE END

Production Notes

The Nutcracker Prince

Number of Puppets: 7 hand or rod puppets or marionettes, including Prince as himself and as Nutcracker. Any number of dancing Candies or Snowflakes, plus other dancers for Chinese dance, Russian dance, Arabian dance, and Waltz of the Flowers.

Playing Time: 20 minutes.

Description of Puppets: King Winter and Queen Blanche are in white with glitter all over them to look like snow. Clara can be in a long nightdress. Prince wears regal clothes and Mouse King has a red cape and a crown between his ears. Sugar Plum Fairy wears glittery pink tights and a small crown. Dancers: Snowflakes may be abstract snowflakes or little people dressed like snowflakes. Candies may be all different kinds of candy — candy canes, gumdrops, etc. For Chinese dance, use one, two or three little mushroom-like people with coolie hats. For Russian dance, two or four fur-hatted and full-bloomered dancers. For Arabian dance, a beautiful lady in veils and full skirt. For Waltz of the Flowers, use stylized dancers like flowers with petals as skirts. The Nutcracker should look like a man, with wide jaws. When Prince Marzipan pops out of Nutcracker's mouth, the effect is created by having Clara and Sugar Plum Fairy stand in front of Nutcracker as they open its mouth, hiding it from sight. The two puppets are exchanged.

Properties: Small nutcracker and toys, swords, silver horn, shoe.

Setting: Scenes 1 and 3: A dark night sky with snowflakes. Scene 2: Clara's living room with a small Christmas tree and a large window at back. Scene 4: Sugar Plum Land, with buildings made of candy.

Lighting: Scenes 1 and 3 are dark, scenes 2 and 4 are bright.

Sound: Use the music from Tchaikovsky's "Nutcracker Suite," as indicated in text. Use only short parts of each number to keep each dance to one or two minutes.

KING OF THE GOLDEN RIVER

Adapted from the story by John Ruskin

Characters

NARRATOR
GLUCK
BENJAMIN BLACK, *Gluck's brother*
CRICKET
WEST WIND
KING OF THE GOLDEN RIVER
TURTLE
DOG
OLD MAN

SCENE 1

TIME: *Long ago, in the evening.*

SETTING: *Interior of cottage. Fireplace with pot hanging over fire is at rear; tables and chairs are at center; window and door to outside are at left.*

AT RISE: GLUCK *is looking out window.* NARRATOR *enters and speaks to audience.*

NARRATOR: Once there were two brothers. The elder was mean and selfish, and the younger, named Gluck, was kind and good and hard working. They lived in a valley, once fertile and green, but now drab and dead. (NARRATOR *exits. Sounds of rain, thunder, and wind are heard.*)

The authors wish to acknowledge Pat Platt as co-author of this play.

GLUCK: My, it is a bad night out. I've never seen it rain so. (*He goes to fireplace.*) Let's see ... have I done all my work? I don't think I've forgotten anything. My elder brother Ben would box my ears if he returned and everything wasn't done. (CRICKET *appears.*)

CRICKET: You've forgotten to sweep, and there are a couple of crumbs I had my eye on.

GLUCK: Crumbs?

CRICKET: Yes. Here they are. Right under the table. I'll just help myself if it's all right with you. Ever since the Golden River dried up, this valley has been desolate and bare. There's been little to eat around here for me, as well as the other animals and townfolk. You and your brother have been lucky to have that wonderful well in your yard to make your gardens grow.

GLUCK: That is true. Help yourself to the crumbs, but don't let my brother catch you.

CRICKET: Thank you. It's a beastly night out. Maybe this storm will help the crops, but my poor wings are soaked through. You wouldn't have a spot for me to dry myself, would you?

GLUCK: I'd be only too pleased to let you stay, but if my brother were to catch you, he'd step on you for sure.

CRICKET (*Fearfully*): This wouldn't be the house of Benjamin Black, would it?

GLUCK: I'm afraid so. He's my brother.

CRICKET: I'll be on my way. Thanks for the crumbs. Don't bother opening the door. I'll just squeeze under. Goodbye. (CRICKET *exits left.*)

GLUCK: I hope he doesn't get washed away. (*Two loud knocks at door are heard.*) It must be the wind. (*Two more knocks are heard.*) No — there it is again. (*He looks out window.*) There's a very strange fellow standing outside the door.

WEST WIND (*From offstage*): Hello! That's not the way to answer the door. I'm wet. Let me in!

GLUCK: I'm very sorry, but I can't. (*To himself*) That little fellow has the longest nose I've ever seen.

WEST WIND: Can't indeed. Why can't you?

GLUCK: My brother, Benjamin, would beat me if I did. What do you want, sir?

WEST WIND: Want? I want to come in where it's warm. Let me in!

GLUCK (*To himself*): He does look very wet. I'll just let him in for a few minutes. (GLUCK *goes to open door. Loud wind sound is heard as* WEST WIND *enters.*)

WEST WIND: Thank you, boy. Never mind your brother. I'll explain to him.

GLUCK: Oh, no! That would be the death of me. You must be gone when he comes home. He'll be here any minute.

WEST WIND (*Peering into pot hanging over fire*): That stew looks very good. Can't you give me a little bit?

GLUCK: I'd like to, but my brother would be furious.

WEST WIND: I'm hungry.

GLUCK: Well — you could have my share.

WEST WIND: You're a good lad. You are staring at me, you know.

GLUCK: Excuse me, sir, but . . .

WEST WIND: I know — I look different. But you see, I'm the West Wind. I can blow a little fellow like you thirty feet into the air. (*He giggles.*)

GLUCK: I hope you won't do that, sir.

WEST WIND: I could blow out your fire! Like this! (*He blows out fire and laughs.*)

GLUCK: Oh, dear. I see that you have. (*Loud banging on door is heard.*) And that's my brother knocking on the front door. When he sees the fire is out, and when he sees you, I'll catch it!

BENJAMIN (*From outside*): Open this door, Gluck! (*Bangs again*)

GLUCK: I'm coming. (*He opens door and* BENJAMIN *enters.*)

BENJAMIN (*Angrily*): You took your time to let me in! (*Points to* WEST WIND) Who's that?

GLUCK: He says he's the West Wind.

WEST WIND: How do you do? (*He bows.*)

BENJAMIN: Who let him in?

GLUCK: I did. He was so wet . . .

BENJAMIN (*To* WEST WIND): Have the goodness to get out before I throw you out.

WEST WIND: Would you turn an old man out on such a cold, wet night?

BENJAMIN: You heard me. Out!

WEST WIND: I'm very hungry.

BENJAMIN: That doesn't concern me. Get out of here before I hit you. (BENJAMIN *raises his hand and* WEST WIND *blows him into corner.*)

WEST WIND (*Laughing*): I wish you a very good night. (*Exits laughing*)

BENJAMIN: Hey! What happened?

GLUCK: He blew you across the room.

BENJAMIN: The impudent fellow. It's all your fault for letting him in.

GLUCK: Please don't beat me, brother.

BENJAMIN: What happened to the fire? I'll fix you. (*Starts toward* GLUCK)

GLUCK: Please, brother, I . . . (*Loud clap of thunder is heard, and sound of storm gets louder.* GLUCK *and* BENJAMIN *rush to window.*)

BENJAMIN: There'll be nothing left of our garden after this rain. The corn is already ruined.

GLUCK: The West Wind must be very angry. He's blowing furiously out there. (*Thunder clap and crashing sound are heard.*)

BENJAMIN: Oh, oh . . . There goes the barn with our stores for the winter. We are ruined! (*Curtain*)

* * * * *

SCENE 2

BEFORE RISE: NARRATOR *enters.*
NARRATOR: And so the brothers were then as poor as the people of the valley. The next day we find the brothers worrying about where their next meal will come from. (NARRATOR *exits as curtains open.*)

* * *

SETTING: *Same as Scene 1 except golden mug is on table.*
AT RISE: GLUCK *and* BENJAMIN *are sitting at table.*

BENJAMIN: It's all your fault. If only you hadn't let the West Wind in! Oh, what am I going to do with you? I should throw you out for good!
GLUCK: I didn't mean any harm.
BENJAMIN: Well, we will have to find gold somehow. (*He picks up* GLUCK's *golden mug and goes to fireplace.*)
GLUCK (*Standing; alarmed*): What are you going to do with my golden mug, Benjamin? You aren't going to melt my golden mug, are you?
BENJAMIN: What does it look like? I need money now that the crops are gone. Don't try to stop me.
GLUCK: Please let me keep the mug. Mother gave it to me! I'll work and earn some money if only you'll spare my mug.
BENJAMIN: The gold from the mug will bring more money than you could make in a year. (*Throws mug into pot*) There now. It's beginning to melt already. You watch until it's melted completely, and then pour the gold into

bars. I'm going to town, but I'll be back soon. And that gold had better be ready. (*He exits.*)

GLUCK: Poor little mug. Now we've nothing left of the family's treasure. How fine it would be if the river were made of gold.

KING OF THE GOLDEN RIVER (*From offstage, behind pot*): Gluck!

GLUCK: Who was that?

KING (*Offstage*): Here I am, Gluck! (GLUCK *looks around room and under table.*) Look in the pot!

GLUCK: It can't be! (*Looks in pot.*)

KING: Pour me out! It's hot in here! (GLUCK *tips pot, and* KING, *dressed all in gold, appears.*) Ah, that's better.

GLUCK: You look like my little mug. Were you my mug, sir?

KING: Of course. And I've been watching you for a very long time.

GLUCK: You have?

KING: I just said so, didn't I? I have magical powers, for I am the King of the Golden River.

GLUCK: You are?

KING: I just told you I was. Listen, boy. You're a good lad and I want to help you. I can make the river turn to gold.

GLUCK: But how can you make the river turn to gold?

KING: If you throw three drops of fresh, pure water from your well into the dry mouth of the river, it will turn to gold. You must also read this enchantment. (*A paper appears.* GLUCK *takes it.*)

GLUCK: But the river is so very far away, and the passage is very rough and dangerous.

KING: That's true. It won't be easy. Are you willing to try?

GLUCK: Indeed I am, sir.

KING: Excellent. Oh, just one thing. If you fail, you'll be turned to stone.

GLUCK: Turned to stone?

KING: That's what I said, didn't I? Are you still willing to try, lad?

GLUCK: We're so poor, I guess I really have no other choice.

KING: Good luck, boy. (*He disappears.*)

GLUCK: Where did he go? (*Looks around*) He just vanished! (*Loud pounding on door is heard.*) Oh, dear. Here comes Benjamin, and I haven't made the gold bars. (*He opens door.*)

BENJAMIN (*Entering*): Have you finished? (*Goes to pot*) Where are the gold bars?

GLUCK: Oh, brother, don't beat me. We'll soon have more gold than we'll know what to do with.

BENJAMIN: Have you lost your senses?

GLUCK: I met the King of the Golden River, and he said if I would take three drops of water from our well and drop them into the mouth of the river, it would turn to gold. I must also read this enchantment at the same time. (*Shows him paper.*)

BENJAMIN: It should be easy to tell if you're lying. I will go myself.

GLUCK: But he said if I failed I would be turned to . . .

BENJAMIN: Never mind about failing. I'll get the well water, and I'll find the mouth of the river. But you had better be telling me the truth.

GLUCK: Be careful, brother. (BENJAMIN *storms out. Curtain*)

*　　*　　*　　*　　*

SCENE 3

BEFORE RISE: NARRATOR *enters.*

NARRATOR: So, off went Benjamin to see if his brother,

Gluck, had told the truth — to see if the river would turn to gold. (NARRATOR *exits as curtains open.*)

*   *   *

SETTING: *Scene of rocky mountain pass is painted on backdrop; dried-up waterfall is at left.*

AT RISE: BENJAMIN *enters, right, carrying jug. He sits.*

BENJAMIN: The sun certainly is hot today. But it won't be long till I reach the mouth of the river. I'm sure glad I filled this jug with cool water. I can drink some since I need only three drops to put into the riverbed. (TURTLE *enters.*) What a silly-looking turtle. Ha, ha — it's all covered with dust.

TURTLE: Please, sir. Could I have a drink of water? I'm parched from the heat.

BENJAMIN: A talking turtle? Ha! Well, he won't be talking long. (*To* TURTLE) Go away from me before I step on you. That'll be the day — when I share my water with a silly talking turtle. (TURTLE *exits slowly.* BENJAMIN *stands and starts left.*) That riverbed should be this way somewhere.

DOG (*Entering*): Woof! Woof! (*Panting*) Please, sir. I am very thirsty. Could I share your water?

BENJAMIN: No, you may not! Nothing but beggars on the road today.

DOG: I'll be your friend if . . .

BENJAMIN: I don't need friends, especially not scrawny, mangy, talking dogs. Get on your way, or I'll throw you down the cliff. (DOG *exits.*)

OLD MAN (*Entering*): Please, sir, may I have a few drops of your water? I haven't had anything to drink all day. I am very thirsty.

BENJAMIN: Get on your way. I don't have enough for myself.

OLD MAN: Just a few drops!

BENJAMIN: I'll give you a push down the hill if you don't move on.

OLD MAN: No, no! I'll be on my way. But beware, Benjamin Black, and goodbye. (OLD MAN *exits.*)

BENJAMIN: Good riddance. (*He drinks from jug*) Ah-h-h! That's refreshing. But I had better leave the rest for the river. (*He continues left till he comes to dried-up waterfall.*) Here is the place. Now, let me see if I remember the enchantment. (*Reciting*)

Into the Golden River bed
Three fresh drops of water are fed
To start the river flowing with gold —
A beautiful sight, riches untold. . . .

Now to pour the water. (*He does. Rumbling sound is heard.*) What's the matter? There is no golden water coming out. I . . . feel funny . . . Something's happening . . . Oh, no . . . I'm turning into stone . . . (*Shouts*) Ah-h-h-h-h! (BENJAMIN *disappears and big black stone with his likeness on it appears in his place. Curtain.*)

*   *   *   *   *

SCENE 4

BEFORE RISE: NARRATOR *enters.*

NARRATOR: Benjamin Black refused to share and the water he poured was made impure by his selfishness. He was turned into a big black stone. After a week, Gluck came to the rocky place to try to find his brother. (NARRATOR *exits as curtains open.*)

*   *   *

SETTING: *Same as Scene 3, including rock representing Benjamin.*

AT RISE: GLUCK *enters right, carrying jug.*

GLUCK (*Calling loudly*): Benjamin! Brother Benjamin! (*To himself*) Where could my brother be? It's been a whole week since he left, and he hasn't come home. Perhaps he has lost his way.

TURTLE (*Entering*): Please, Gluck, could I have a drink of water? I'm parched from the heat.

GLUCK: Oh, you poor, little, dried-up thing. Of course. I have plenty. (*He gives* TURTLE *water.*)

TURTLE: You are most kind, Gluck. (*He ambles offstage.*)

GLUCK: He knew my name. Wait! He was talking. Amazing!

DOG (*Entering*): Woof! Woof! (*Panting*) Please, Gluck. I am very thirsty. Could I share your water?

GLUCK: Another talking animal! (*To* DOG) There is still enough water in the jug. By all means you may have some. Here, you poor doggie. (DOG *drinks.*) You sure were thirsty.

DOG: I will always be your friend, Gluck. Thank you. (DOG *exits.*)

GLUCK: And a sweet friend he will be, too. (*Looks in jug*) Oh, my — just a little water left.

OLD MAN (*Entering*): Please, Gluck, may I have a few drops of your water? I haven't had anything to drink all day.

GLUCK: What shall I do? Poor old man. I have only a few drops left, but I am willing to share them with you.

OLD MAN: You will not be sorry, Gluck. (*He drinks.*) Delicious. You are very generous. Now I must be on my way. Goodbye, Gluck. (*He exits.* GLUCK *crosses left.*)

GLUCK: There's the river's mouth. I still have a few drops of water left. I hope there is enough. Now, let's see. How did the enchantment go? Oh, yes. (*Reciting*)

> Into the Golden River bed
> Three fresh drops of water are fed
> To start the river flowing with gold —
> A beautiful sight, riches untold. . . .

Now to pour the water. (*He does. Rumbling sound is heard.*) Something is happening! (*Silver lamé cloth, representing water, comes through hole in backdrop where waterfall is.*) How beautiful! How wonderful! Fresh, cool water! (*He laughs with joy.*)

KING (*Appearing*): Are you disappointed that the water isn't golden?

GLUCK: This is better than gold. Now the valley will be green again, and the fields will yield food for all the people. (*Laughs*)

KING: You are a good boy, Gluck, to think of all your friends and neighbors. I promise my river will never dry up again. (*Gold lamé cloth is pushed through hole so waterfall appears golden.*)

GLUCK: Look! The sun has come from behind a cloud and has made the water look like gold. It's a golden river after all!

KING: Goodbye, Gluck. Always be kind and thoughtful — and remember me!

GLUCK: Goodbye, King of the Golden River. (KING *disappears. Curtain*)

THE END

Production Notes

KING OF THE GOLDEN RIVER

Number of Puppets: 8 hand puppets or marionettes.

Characters: 1 male or female for Narrator.

Playing Time: 20 minutes.

Description of Puppets: Gluck is young and has fair hair. Benjamin is older, has dark hair and beard, and looks mean. King of the Golden River is a dwarf, dressed in shining gold. West Wind has long nose and wears strips of sparkling, green and blue, wispy material. Old Man wears tattered monk's robe with hood over his head. Cricket, Turtle and Dog are of equal size to other puppets.

Properties: Jug; big, black stone (cut-out) with Benjamin's face drawn on it; enchantment paper; golden mug.

Setting: Scene 1 is inside cottage. Fireplace with pot hanging over fire is at rear; rough, wooden table and chairs are at center; window with shabby curtains is at left, as is door. Fireplace should have opening behind it for King of the Golden River to appear from, or pot should be large enough to put King into. In Scene 2, golden mug is placed on table. Scene 3 has painting of rocky mountain pass and river on backdrop. Dried-up waterfall is pictured at left with hole at top so that silver and gold lamé material can be pushed through to represent water, as indicated in Scene 4. Stone with Benjamin's face is onstage throughout Scene 4.

Lighting: Scene 1, lighting is dark and gloomy.

Sound: Knocking, rain, thunder, wind, crashing and rumbling sounds, as indicated in text.